# The Authorities

*Powerful Wisdom from Leaders in the Field*

## ANGELA GOLDEN BRYAN

#1 Bestselling Author & Master Encourager

# FOREWORD

Experts are to be admired for their knowledge, but they often remain unrecognized by the general public because they save their information and insights for paying customers and clients. There are many experts in a given field, but their impact is limited to the handful of people with whom they work.

Unlike experts, authorities share their knowledge and expertise far more broadly, so they make a big impact on the world. Authorities become known and admired as leading experts and, as such, typically do very well economically and professionally. Most authorities are also mature enough to know that part of the joy of monetary success is the accompanying moral and spiritual obligation to give back.

Many people want to learn and work with well-respected and generous authorities, but don't always know where to find them. They may be known to their peers, or within a specific community, but have not had the opportunity to reach a wider audience. At one time, they might have submitted a proposal to the For Dummies or Chicken Soup for the Soul series of books, but it's now almost impossible to get accepted as a new author in such branded book series.

It is more than fitting that Raymond Aaron, an internationally known and respected authority in his own right, would be the one to recognize the need for a new venue in which authorities could share their considerable knowledge with readers everywhere. As the only author ever to be included in both of the book series mentioned above, Raymond has had the opportunity to give back and he understands how crucial it is for authorities to have a platform from which to share their expertise.

I have known and worked with Raymond for a number of years and consider him a valued friend and talented coach. He knows how to spot talented and knowledgeable people and he desires to see them prosper. Over the years, success coaching and speaking engagements around the world have made it possible for Raymond to meet many of these talented authorities. He recognizes and relates to their passion and enthusiasm for what they do, as well as their desire to share what they know. He tells me that's why he created this new nonfiction branded book series, *The Authorities*.

Dr. Nido Qubein
*President, High Point University*

# TABLE OF CONTENTS

# INTRODUCTION

Welcome to *The Authorities*. This is an anthology of stories and ideas from individuals who have distinguished themselves in life and in business. They are people who leave big footprints on the world, and as leaders in their particular fields they also understand the importance and obligation of giving something back.

Authorities are not just experts. They are also known to be outstanding in their fields and in their communities. Because of this important difference, authorities are able to contribute more to humanity through both their chosen work and by giving back.

You will definitely know some of *The Authorities* in this book, especially since there are some world-famous ones. Others are just as exceptional, but you may not yet know about them.

Our featured author, for example, is Angela Golden Bryan. Angela is an actor, writer, professional speaker and producer. For over 20 years Angela has performed on stage, as well as on television and film. She grew up on the beautiful island of St. Croix, which is part of the US Virgin Islands. Her passion for storytelling and human rights merged in her groundbreaking project sharing and recounting the Fireburn labor revolt of 1878. The Fireburn is an important, yet not widely known, part of African Diaspora, Danish, Caribbean, and US history. Part of Angela's mission is to change that.

Angela wrote "Fireburn the Screenplay: A Story of Passion Ignited Based on the History of St. Croix" which made the Amazon #1 bestseller list in 2019. She then went on to release "James and the Fireburn: An Anti-bullying and Human Rights Story Inspired by Caribbean History" which is the award winning children's book based on her son's experience of being bullied. Angela presents a strong anti-bullying message while teaching children a bit about history. Angela is the executive producer of "Fireburn The Documentary" which takes a deeper look at the folklore, tradition, and history surrounding the Fireburn of 1878.

Angela is proud to be an ambassador for Human Rights with the United Nations Association-USA, Broward County, FL chapter. She is passionate about people being treated with respect and dignity, and believes that each of us has a great opportunity to change the world by sharing love not only with our friends and family, but with the world as a whole. This passion has led her to sharing steps you can take to live a more love centered life. She came to realize that love is indeed the answer and can be the jumping off point to solving many problems. If you want to live a life grounded in passionate love for not only others but yourself, Angela has some wonderful advice for you and your loved ones. She strives to work on her "love walk" every day and hopes you will be inspired to do the same.

Visit www.AngelaGoldenBryan.com for more information or connect with Angela at AngelaGoldenBryan@gmail.com.

We suggest you read each chapter carefully to learn and to see the business possibilities that may exist between yourself and any of *The Authorities*. You could become their client or, perhaps, do business with them in other ways.

These are *The Authorities*. Learn from them. Connect with them. Let them uplift you. Learning from them and working with them is a secret ingredient for success which may well allow you to rise to the level of Authority soon.

To be considered for inclusion in a subsequent edition of *The Authorities*, register to attend an event at www.aaron.com/events where you will be interviewed and considered.

# What the World Needs Now

## How to Cultivate More Love in Your Life and Change the World

### ANGELA GOLDEN BRYAN

*"What the world needs now is love, sweet love*

*It's the only thing that there's just too little of*

*What the world needs now is love, sweet love,*

*No not just for some but for everyone..."*

- Jackie DeShannon

S ometimes it may seem like the world is filled with negativity and chaos. No matter who you are or where you live, the world around you can change overnight. Perhaps it was already evolving slowly, but you were too busy to notice or didn't want to acknowledge it. When the world seems to be spinning out of control, remember that, despite the anxiety, frustration, and negativity, we all have the choice as to how we will respond to it. You may not be able to control the world around you, but you can manage your thoughts better. My first introduction to this life-changing truth occurred in high school when I read Viktor Frankl's groundbreaking book, "Man's Search for Meaning." Frankl was imprisoned in a concentration camp during WWII and experienced daily physical, verbal, and emotional abuse. Although he faced uncertainty, and even death, during that horrific time, he survived by realizing he still had control over his thoughts. Frankl developed techniques that helped him choose positive thoughts over negative ones. After reading this compelling book, it was clear to me that choosing to discipline my mind, and not have it controlled by outward circumstances, was an essential key to finding personal happiness, joy, and fulfillment.

## THE IMPORTANCE OF OUR THOUGHTS IN TIMES OF CRISIS

While I'm writing this, we are living through an unprecedented time in modern history. The world is in the throes of the COVID -19 pandemic and there are worldwide anti-racist protests calling for systemic change. On the occasions that I tune into the media, scenes of growing fear, hatred, rage, and anxiety confront me. Misinformation is also spreading, and much of it adds to the feeling of chaos and despair for many. What I know to be true is that what we think controls our feelings and emotions, which leads to our actions. Our actions include how we interact with others, as well as ourselves.

Some daily tools that help me to maintain healthy thoughts are praying, reading Scripture, and saying affirmations. When I use the word "affirmation," I am referring to an encouraging statement, based on God's truth and how he sees me and my circumstances. For example, if I'm feeling fearful and lonely, I might repeat the following affirmation: "God is always with me, he gives me courage." I based this affirmation on the Bible verse: "Be strong and courageous. Do not be afraid or terrified because of them, for the Lord your God goes with you; he will never leave you nor forsake you." (NIV, Deuteronomy 31:6) When I habitually practice these strategies, I tend to have more positive thoughts, feel better about myself, others, and life, and my actions are more conducive to health. This practice has come in handy when confronted by simple tasks that now have the capacity to be a bit stressful due to the current events.

One example is venturing out to buy groceries. Once, after enjoying a car ride filled with upbeat songs and affirmations, I entered the market feeling energized and joy-filled. However, I noticed that the workers weren't their usual cheerful selves. Instead, they seemed subdued and did not engage in their customary "small talk." Before I knew what was happening, I burst into song. The song that came to me was a hit from many years ago: "What the world needs now is love, sweet love. It's the only thing that there's just too little of..." I wasn't even through a third of the song when a few people joined in, and together we sang this happy tune about love being "the only thing that there's just too little of." It felt like a scene out of a Broadway musical. We laughed and smiled, knowing we had brightened the atmosphere.

Reflecting on my experience while driving home, I felt grateful to be part of such a fun and loving experience. (And with strangers no less!) However, a line from the song continued to loop through my mind "… it's the only thing that there's just too little of." Was it true? Is there a love shortage? Are people hoarding love as opposed to giving it away? Are people selling their love to the highest bidder?

"What the world needs now is love…" Truer words have never been spoken. The world is hurting and needs love; however, I refuse to believe that there isn't enough love to go around. I think that perhaps we've forgotten how to love. I encourage you to find love within yourself and learn how to cultivate and share it. Let's start with those closest and spread our love to the world, one person at a time. I believe in your capacity to love and look forward to being a part of your "love journey." Let's examine what love is, take a look at the part forgiveness plays, and step onto a clearer path back to LOVE.

## HOW DO WE DEFINE LOVE?

We all use the word "love" in our everyday life. You may express it to someone by saying, "I love you" or exclaim that you "love" something. But have you ever stopped and asked yourself how you'd define love? Curious, I went online and searched: "What is the best definition of love?" The following answers came up in my search: "The most spectacular, indescribable, deep euphoric feeling for someone; love is an incredibly powerful word; love is unconditional affection with no limits or conditions; (love is) when you trust the other with your life and when you would do anything for each other."

Next, I sought an answer from the Bible. Here is 1 Corinthians' description: "Love is patient, love is kind. It does not envy, it does not boast; it is not proud. It does not dishonor others, it is not self-seeking, it is not easily angered, it keeps no record of wrongs. Love does not delight in evil but rejoices with the truth.  It always protects, always trusts, always hopes, always perseveres." (NIV, 1 Corinthians 13:4-7)

Both online and in the Bible, love is the grand undertaking. Words such as "no limits and conditions" as well as "always," may create a feeling of immense pressure around what love is. I don't know that I can "always" love, or love without "limits and conditions," but I do believe it is worth trying! Perhaps the best place to start is to examine what love is not.

## WHAT LOVE IS NOT

I believe that all of us are familiar with the face of "unloving." Unloving is the opposite of love, even though some try to pass it off as love. I have seen my fair share of it, and have acted in unloving ways on more than one occasion. Some prime examples are controlling others, manipulation, jealousy, obsession, lack of boundaries, and codependency. Love goes beyond romantic relationships and includes all manner of partnerships and alliances (including the one you have with yourself). Based on 1 Corinthians 13:4-7, we see that love does not: encourage envy, dishonor others, keep a record of wrongs, or delight in evil. We also understand that love is not: proud, self-seeking, or easily angered. All of the actions and states of being mentioned above stem from fear and show us what the opposite of love is. To move towards being a more loving person, we must eliminate these unloving behaviors. The process may be challenging, and you may come up against years of negative thought patterns. However, just imagine the rewards you will reap by doing this work!

The laws of physics tell us that nature abhors a void, so if a vacuum exists, something will fill it. If we are not intentional about what fills a space, something less than desirable may "sneak" in and fill it. This law is seen in nature and is no less visible in our personal lives. I do not have what some call a "green thumb;" however, I have grown potted herbs over the years. On more than one occasion, I've purchased pots, soil, and seeds, began the process, only to get side tracked. After putting dirt in a container, I got distracted and left it untended for a few days. When I finally came back, weeds were growing out of the pots. I had not planted "weed" seeds, but they found their way into my untended soil! So it is in life; weeds of negativity spring up without our intentionally planting them. If you want love to fill the void, it is essential to be intentional about "planting" seeds of love. Often, we must first uproot weeds before we can replace them with love. To choose love, we must recognize love. If we don't know what love looks like, we may settle for weeds of negativity, which grow into unhealthy thoughts, emotions, and finally, behaviors.

## WHAT IS LOVE?

If you define what love is and make it personal, you will have the power to invite more of it into your life. Referring back to 1 Corinthians 13:4-7, love is: patient and kind, and it protects, trusts, hopes, perseveres, and rejoices with the truth. These loving qualities will be most welcome into your life when you are willing to release fear, greed, envy, competition, expectation, judgment, and a critical spirit. As we release the non-supportive and negative thoughts, emotions, and actions, we learn to love ourselves and others more. You will find that, every time you are willing to let something go, you will open yourself up to new possibilities. When you release the expectation that you, or others, need to be perfect, you will cultivate more patience. When you treat others as you would like to be treated, you are more kind and, in turn, invite more kindness into your life. When you release the fear of rejection, abandonment, and being cheated, you will trust more. All these actions will bring more love into your life because these positive actions are ways that we love. We find the strength to make these changes in God. By trusting God, you will persevere, and love will flourish in your life.

## PERSONALIZED LOVE

While it's helpful to discuss what love is or is not, it is also essential to keep in mind that love looks different based on each person's personality. The truth that "love is kind" may mean giving a hug to the personality type that is motivated by relationships. In contrast, it may mean contributing to household chores for the goal-oriented personality type. In my workshops, I help people discover their unique personality blends, which brings clarity to how they see themselves and others. This clarity takes the "puzzle" out of relationships and frees individuals to love on a personal, authentic level. This simple process can be life-changing.

The starting point is understanding that everyone is not like you, and you're not like anyone else. From this healthy model of personality, we also understand that being different is not bad; it's just different. With this in mind, we know that love will look and feel different for each individual. Everyone is unique, so it makes sense that giving and receiving love may not look the same to those around you.

I have taught personality profiles to couples, teens, corporate teams, and women's groups for better understanding relationships. It is exciting to see lightbulbs go off in people's minds as they come to understand why they have experienced a feeling of disconnect in particular relationships, be it at work, home, houses of worship, or school. Everyone expresses and receives love in unique ways, which may be different from our own. It is of great value to understand your personality blend so that you will have more empowered relationships with everyone. Contact me directly at AngelaGoldenBryan. com to set up a free consultation to see if my "Solving Your People Puzzles" workshop is right for you, your family, or business.

## RETURNING TO LOVE

When returning to love, you must first become aware of behaviors that block you from love. One of my mentors, Dr. Robert Rohm, says, "We cannot beware of something until we are first aware of it." It makes sense, doesn't it?

Once you are aware of the behaviors keeping you from love, the next step is to release these behaviors. As previously mentioned in 1 Corinthians 13:4-7, negative mindsets such as envy or being easily angered keep us from love. To release the fears associated with competition, sense of lack, judgment, manipulation, control, unforgiveness, and revenge, we must see ourselves as God sees us. Seeing ourselves as God sees us, as well as seeing others as God sees them, is a vital part of the path to love. When we understand that God made us in His image and that we each have a purpose for being here, we come closer to learning how to love more deeply.

## HOW GOD FEELS ABOUT YOU AND LOVE

"The mountains and hills may crumble, but my love for you will never end." (GNT, Isaiah 54:10) When you ground yourself in God's love, you set yourself up to love others, even in challenging times. It's easier to be a loving person when you understand and remember why God loves you. Feeling God's love will remove fears, and as previously mentioned, there is more room for love when there is less fear in your life. Pastor Rick Warren gave some crucial reminders of what God thinks of us in one of his daily devotionals. Here are a few of my favorites that help me remember why and how to love.

## God Accepts You as You Are:

"Jesus . . . made us acceptable to God." (CEV, Titus 3:7) No matter what you've done or what you do, by dying on the cross, Jesus has made us entirely justifiable to God. We are "right" with God. We spend a lot of time trying to gain the acceptance of others, but what matters is that you are already accepted fully by God.

## God Loves You Unconditionally:

God doesn't say, "I love you if . . ." or "I love you because . . ." He says, "I love you—period!" You can't make God stop loving you, because his love is not based on what you do but on who he is. God's reassurance of this truth states: "The mountains and hills may crumble, but my love for you will never end." (GNT, Isaiah 54:10)

## God Wholeheartedly Forgives You:

God doesn't rehearse your sins; he releases them because they are done and over with. Jesus died on the cross and gave his life as a sacrifice for your sins. Jesus' sacrificial death means that you are forgiven when you accept the gift of forgiveness from God. Romans 8:1 puts it this way: "There is no condemnation for those who belong to Christ Jesus." (NLT)

## You're Valuable in God's Sight:

You are a child of God and "have been bought and paid for by Christ"

(TLB, 1 Corinthians 7:23) Jesus Christ paid for your life by offering his own life. The price that someone is willing to pay for something is often indicative of how valuable it is. Jesus' life is the highest price ever paid – that makes you priceless!

Remember that it is not about what you or others think about yourself; it is about what God thinks about you.

# FORGIVENESS

One of the main blocks to cultivating more love in your life is holding on to resentment and not being able to forgive. Forgiveness is critical in bringing joy and growth to your life. What you must realize is that not being able to forgive will harm you more than the offender. I've heard it said many times, and I'll repeat it here: Holding on to resentment is like drinking poison and expecting the other person to die!

Forgiveness is when we choose to let go of feelings of resentment or anger against another when we feel hurt, rejected, or treated poorly by them. We must forgive, whether we believe the other person deserves it or not. Remember that when you forgive, it doesn't mean you condone their behavior. It also doesn't mean that you have to maintain a relationship with them, especially if they are a threat to your safety and wellbeing. When you forgive, you follow God's example because he forgave you.

When you don't forgive others, you affect your emotional and physical wellbeing, often without realizing it. Many of us have seen the pain and suffering that unforgiveness brings the unforgiving individual. I have also experienced this pain, and so it is with love and understanding that I encourage you to forgive and make space for love. Your health and happiness depend on it. Learning to forgive is crucial for your wellbeing!

# STEPS TO FORGIVENESS

Although I present several steps to forgiveness in this chapter, I encourage you to embrace the fact that forgiveness is a process and may have a timeline of its own, regardless of how sincere you are. The desire to forgive may be there, yet you might still feel that "niggling" feeling in your stomach. Anger, resentment, and even rage may threaten to rise to the surface. If this happens, don't give up. Keep at it until there isn't a "knee-jerk" response to the individual you are seeking to forgive. Repeat the steps, pray for God to help you forgive, and be patient with yourself.  You will get there if that is your desire, and you are taking the active steps towards forgiveness.

**Revisit the Occasion of "Offense":** Be willing to think about the events that led to your feeling hurt or resentful.  Think about your past reaction as well as how you currently feel. How has it affected your mind, mood, or actions?

**Role Play:** Imagine how the other person may have felt or what they may have been thinking. When you do this, you are exercising empathy. Empathy is invaluable when going through the process of forgiveness. Being mindful of other people's stories and histories can help you connect with the bigger picture, and discover possible reasons why the conflict has arisen. It may not be 100% their fault. Remember that no one is perfect, including yourself.

**Release Attachment to the End Result:** When going through the process of forgiveness, do not be attached to a specific outcome or action from the other person. For example, although you desire it, apologies or reconciliations may not occur between you and the person you are working on forgiving.

**Be Intentional by Choosing to Forgive:** Choosing to forgive another is one of the most liberating decisions you can make. It doesn't have to occur in a conversation; it can be as simple as writing about it in a journal or even talking to someone you trust.

**Include Yourself:** Forgiving yourself is as crucial as forgiving others. All of us have had moments in our lives that we are not proud of, and we've all made mistakes. It is just as essential to go through the forgiveness process with yourself so that you can let go of resentment and anger, thereby allowing more room for love.

# FILLING YOUR LIFE WITH LOVE

"Keep company with him and learn a life of love. Observe how Christ loved us. His love was not cautious but extravagant. He didn't love to get something from us but to give everything of himself to us. Love like that." ( MSG, Ephesians 5:2)

Becoming a loving person will not happen overnight. It is a process, but a worthwhile one that will change you and your relationships forever. I have followed Joyce Meyer's teachings for years, and I admire her authentic teachings on love. Without shame for her failures, she shares her love journey in a way that only she can do.  Here are some practical tips on where to start:

- Learn how mature love acts and responds by reflecting God's word.

- Dedicate the first 10 minutes of your day to reflect on love and ask for God's help.

- Memorize Scripture focusing on love so that you can easily refer to it in trying times.

- Love is a muscle that needs strengthening, so practice!

- Join a small group of people that are dedicated to filling their life with more love.

As I continue to apply these teachings to my life, my capacity to love increases. Each day that I commit to working on my "love walk," I get better. I invite you to do the same.

## LOVE IS A SKILL

When developing a new skill, you first have to decide that you want to learn. After that decision you must be willing to dedicate your time to developing that skill. Love is a skill that you can develop and grow. It's not fair to expect that you will be a master at loving right away. But know that you can be a better lover than you are now. Practicing love and getting better at it is what God wants of you. God wants you to be a master when it comes to love! Like any new skill, the growth curve may feel awkward, and you may encounter many setbacks on your path to mastery. But setbacks are never a reason to give up, because every master was once a disaster! Trust that you will gain confidence, and with God on your side, you will have the power to become an expert at love.

I can only write based on my experience and I come to you knowing that God is my Father; Jesus is his Son, and he died for my sins; and that the Holy Spirit empowers and comforts me. This is the foundational truth upon which this chapter is written.  If you don't have a personal relationship with Jesus, please join me by saying this simple, yet life-changing prayer:

*Dear Heavenly Father,*

*I know that I am not perfect and have missed the mark. I have sinned and I am sorry and ask for your forgiveness. I believe Jesus died on the cross and that he rose from the dead, and is alive today. I surrender and ask Jesus to be my Savior and live in my heart and my life. I thank you for accepting me just as I am, and for loving me enough to not let me stay this way. I believe you are now my Savior and that the Holy Spirit lives in me. Thank you, Father. Amen.*

For more inspiration, healthy lifestyle tips, and fun, connect with me online. I look forward to journeying with you, one love-step at a time, as we live our God-given purpose together!

**AngelaGoldenBryan.com**
**www.instagram.com/AngelaGoldenBryan**
**youtube.com/c/AngelaGoldenBryan**

# Step Into Greatness

LES BROWN

Y ou have greatness within you. You can do more than you could ever imagine. The problem most people have is that they set a goal and then ask "how can I do it? I don't have the necessary skills or education or experience".

I know what that's like. I wasted 14 years on asking myself how I could be a motivational speaker. My mind focused on the negative—on the things that were in my way, rather than on the things that were not.

It's not what you don't have but what you think you need that keeps you from getting what you want from life. But, when the dream is big enough, the obstacles don't matter. You'll get there if you stay the course. Nothing can stop you but death itself.

Think about that last statement for a minute. There's nothing on this earth that can stop you from achieving what it is that you want. So, get out of your way, and quit sabotaging your dreams. Do everything in your power to make them happen—because you cannot fail!

They say the best way to die is with your loved ones gathered around your bed. But what if you were dying and it was the ideas you never acted upon, the gifts you never used and the dreams you never pursued, that were circled around your bed? Answer that question right now. Write down your answers. If you die this very moment what ideas, what gifts, what dreams will die with you?

Then say: I refuse to die an unlived life! You beat out 40 million sperm to get here, and you'll never have to face such odds again. Walk through the field of life and leave a trail behind.

One day, one of my rich friends brought my mother a new pair of shoes for me. Now, even though we weren't well off, I didn't want them; they were a size nine and I was a size nine and a half. My mother didn't listen and told my sister to go get some Vaseline, which she rubbed all over my feet. Then my mother had me put those shoes on, minding that I didn't scrunch down the heel. She had my sister run some water in the bathtub, and I was told to get in and walk around in the water. I said that my feet hurt. She just ignored me and asked about my day at school, how everything went and did I get into any fights? I knew what she was up to, that she was trying to distract me, so I said I had only gotten into three fights. After a while mother asked me if my feet still hurt. I admitted that the pain had indeed lessened. She kept me walking in that tub until I had a brand new pair of comfortable, size nine and a half shoes.

You see, once the leather in the shoes got wet, they stretched! And what you need to do is stretch a little. I believe that most people don't set high goals and miss them, but rather, they set lower goals and hit them and then they stay there, stuck on the side of the highway of life. When you're pursuing your greatness, you don't know what your limitations are, and you need to act like you don't have any. If you shoot for the moon and miss, you'll still be in the stars.

You also need coaching (a mentor). Why? There are times you, too, will find yourself parked on the side of the highway of life with no gas in the vehicle. What you need then is someone to stop and offer to pick up some gas down the road a ways and bring it back to you. That person is your coach. Yes, they are there for advice, but their main job is to help you through the difficulties that life throws at all of us.

Another reason for having a coach is that you can't see the picture when you're in the frame. In other words, he or she can often see where you are with a clarity and focus that's unavailable to you. They're not going to leave you parked along the road of life, nor are they going to allow you to be stuck in the moment like a photo in a frame.

And let's say you just can't see your way forward. You don't believe it's possible. Sometimes you just have to believe in someone's belief in you. This could be your coach, a loved one or even a staunch friend. You need to hear them say you can do it, time and again. Because, after all, faith comes from hearing and hearing and hearing.

Look at it this way. Most people fail because of possibility blindness. They can't see what lies before them. There are always possibilities. Because of this, your dream is possible. You may fail often. In fact, I want you to say this: I will fail my way to success. Here is why.

I had a TV show that failed. I felt I had to go back to public speaking. I had failed, so I parked my car for ten years. Then I saw Dr. Wayne Dyer was still on PBS and I decided to call them. They said they would love to work with me and asked where I had been. I wasn't as good as I had been ten years before, as I was out of practice, but I still had to get back in the game. I was determined to drive on empty.

Listen to recordings, go to seminars, challenge yourself, and you'll begin to step into your greatness, you'll begin to fill yourself with the energy you need to climb to greater heights. Most people never attend a seminar. They won't invest money in books or audio programs. You put yourself in the top 5 percent just by making a different choice than the average person. This is called contrary thinking. It's a concept taken from the financial industry. One considers choosing the exact opposite behaviour of the average person as a way to get better than average results. You don't have to make the contrarian choice, but if you don't have anything to lose by going that road, why not consider the option?

Make your move before you're ready. Walk by faith not by sight and make sure you're happy doing it. If you can't be happy, what else is there? Helen Keller said, "Life is short, eat the dessert first."

What is faith? Many of us think of God when we think of faith. A different viewpoint claims that faith is a firm belief in something for which there is no proof. I would rather think of faith as something that is believed especially with strong conviction. It is this last definition I am referring to when I say walk by faith not by sight. Be happy and go forth with strong conviction that you are destined for greatness.

An important step on your way to greatness is to take the time to detoxify. You've got to look at the people in your life. What are they doing for you? Are they setting a pace that you can follow? If not, whose pace have you adjusted to? If you're the smartest in your group, find a new group.

Are the people in your life pulling you down or lifting you up? You know what to do, right? Banish the negative and stay with the positive; it's that simple. Dr. Norman Vincent Peale once said (when I was in the audience), "You are special. You have greatness within you, and you can do more than you could ever possibly imagine."

He overrode the inner conversations in my mind and reached the heart of me. He set me on fire. This is yet another reason for seeking out the help of a coach or mentor or other new people in your life. They can do what Dr. Peale did for me. They can set your passion free.

How important is it to have the right kind of person/people on your side? There was a study done that determined it takes 16 people saying you can do something to overcome one person who says you can't do something. That's right, one negative, unsupportive person can wipe out the work of 16 other supportive people. The message can't be any clearer than that.

Let's face the cold, hard truth: most people stay in park along the highway of life. They never feel the passion, the love for their fellow man, or for the work they do. They are stuck in the proverbial rut. What's the reason? There are many reasons, but only one common factor: fear — fear of change, fear of failure, fear of success, fear they may not be good enough, fear of competition, even fear of rejection.

"Rejection is a myth," says Jack Canfield, co-author of The Chicken Soup for the Soul series. "It's not like you get a slap in the face each time you are rejected." Why not take every "no" you receive as a vitamin, and every time you take one know you are another step closer to success.

You will win if you don't quit. Even a broken clock is right twice a day.

Professional baseball players, on average, get on base just three times out of every ten times they face the opposing pitcher. Even superstars fail half of the time they appear at the plate.

Top commissioned salespeople face similar odds. They may make one sale from every three people they see, but it will have taken them between 75 and 100 telephone calls to make the 15 appointments they need to close their five sales for the week. And these are statistics for the elite. Most salespeople never reach these kinds of numbers.

People don't spend their lives working for just one company anymore. This means you must build up a set of skills and experiences that are portable. This can be done a number of ways, but my favourite approaches follow.

You must be willing to do the things others won't do in order to have tomorrow the things that others don't have. Provide more service than you get paid for. Set some high standards for yourself.

Begin each day with your most difficult task. The rest of the day will seem more enjoyable and a whole lot easier.

Someone needs help with a problem? Be the solution to that problem.

Also, find those tasks that are being consistently ignored and do them. You'll be surprised by the results. An acquaintance of mine used this approach at a number of entry-level positions and each time he quickly ended up being offered a position in management.

You must increase your energy. Kick it up a notch. We are spirits having a physical existence; let your spirit shine. Quit frittering away your energy. Use it to move you closer to the achievement of your dreams. Refuse to spend it on non-productive activities.

What do people say about you when you leave a room? Are you willing to take responsibility—to walk your talk. There is a terrible epidemic sweeping our nation, and it is the refusal to take responsibility for one's actions. Consider that at some point in any situation there will have been a moment where you could have done something to change the outcome. To that end you are responsible for what happened. It's a hard thing to accept, but it's true.

Life's hard. It was hard when I was told I had cancer. I had sunken into despair, and was hiding away in my study when my son came in. My son asked me if I was going to die. What could I do? I told him I was going to fight, even though I was scared. I also told him that I needed some help. Not because I was weak but because I wanted to stay strong. Keep asking until you get help. Don't stop until you get it.

A setback is the setup for a comeback. A setback is simply a misstep on the long road of success. It means nothing in the larger scheme of things. And, surprisingly, it sets you up for your next win. It tends to focus you and your energy on your immediate goals, paving the way for your next sprint, for your comeback.

It's worth it. Your dreams are worth the sacrifices you'll have to make to achieve them. Find five reasons that will make your dreams worth it for you. Say to yourself, I refuse to live an unlived life.

If you are casual about your dreams, you'll end up a casualty. You must be passionate about your dreams, living and breathing them throughout your days. You've got to be hungry! People who are hungry refuse to take no for an answer. Make NO your vitamin. Be ^ IGone, But Not Without Hope. Be hungry.

Let me give you an example of what I mean by hungry …

I decided I wanted to become a disc jockey, so I went down to the local radio station and asked the manager, Mr. Milton "Butterball" Smith, if he had a job available for a disc jockey. He said he did not. The next day I went back, and Mr. Smith asked "Weren't you here yesterday?" I explained that I was just checking to see if anyone was sick or had died. He responded by telling me not to come back again. Day three, I went back again—with the same story. Mr. Smith told me to get out of there. I came back the fourth day and gave Mr. Smith my story one more time. He was so beside himself that he told me to get him a cup of coffee. I said, "Yes, sir!" That's how I became the errand boy.

While working as an errand boy at the station, I took every opportunity to hang out with the deejays and to observe them working. After I had taught myself how to run the control room, it was just a matter of biding my time.

Then one day an opportunity presented itself. One of the disc jockeys by the name of Rockin' Roger was drinking heavily while he was on the air. It was a Saturday afternoon. And there I was, the only one there.

I watched him through the control-room window. I walked back and forth in front of that window like a cat watching a mouse, saying "Drink, Rock, Drink!" I was young. I was ready. And I was hungry.

Pretty soon, the phone rang. It was the station manager. He said, "Les, this is Mr. Klein."

I said, "Yes, I know."

He said, "Rock can't finish his program."

I said, "Yes sir, I know."

He said, "Would you call one of the other disc jockeys to fill in?"

I said, "Yes sir, I sure will, sir."

And when he hung up, I said, "Now he must think I'm crazy." I called up my mama and my girlfriend, Cassandra, and I told them, "Ya'll go out on the front porch and turn up the radio, I'M ABOUT TO COME ON THE AIR!"

I waited 15 or 20 minutes and called the station manager back. I said, "Mr. Klein, I can't find NOBODY!"

He said, "Young boy, do you know how to work the controls?"

I said, "Yes, sir."

He said, "Go in there, but don't say anything. Hear me?"

I said, "Yes, sir."

I couldn't wait to get old Rock out of the way. I went in there, took my seat behind that turntable, flipped on the microphone and let 'er rip.

"Look out, this is me, LB., triple P. Les Brown your platter-playin' papa. There were none before me and there will be none after me, therefore that makes me the one and only. Young and single and love to mingle, certified, bona fide and indubitably qualified to bring you satisfaction and a whole lot of action. Look out baby, I'm your LOVE man."

I WAS HUNGRY!

During my adult life I've been a deejay, a radio station manager, a Democrat in the Ohio Legislature, a minister, a TV personality, an author and a public speaker, but I've always looked after what I valued most—my mother. What I want for her is one of my dreams, one of my goals.

My life has been a true testament to the power of positive thinking and the infinite human potential. I was born in an abandoned building on a floor in Liberty City, a low-income section of Miami, Florida, and adopted at six weeks of age by Mrs. Mamie Brown, a 38-year-old single woman, cafeteria cook and domestic worker. She had very little education or financial means, but a very big heart and the desire to care for myself and my twin brother. I call myself Mrs. Mamie Brown's Baby Boy and I say that all that I am and all that I ever hoped to be, I owe to my mother.

My determination and persistence in searching for ways to help my mother overcome poverty and developing my philosophy to do whatever it takes to achieve success led me to become a distinguished authority on harnessing human potential and success. That philosophy is best expressed by the following …

"If you want a thing bad enough to go out and fight for it,

to work day and night for it,

to give up your time, your peace and your sleep for it…

if all that you dream and scheme is about it,

and life seems useless and worthless without it…

if you gladly sweat for it and fret for it and plan for it

and lose all your terror of the opposition for it…

if you simply go after that thing you want

with all of your capacity, strength and sagacity,

faith, hope and confidence and stern pertinacity…

if neither cold, poverty, famine, nor gout,

sickness nor pain, of body and brain,

can keep you away from the thing that you want…

if dogged and grim you beseech and beset it,

with the help of God, you will get it!"

# Branding Small Business

RAYMOND AARON

Branding is an incredibly important tool for creating and building your business. Large companies have been benefiting from branding ever since people first started selling things to other people. Branding made those businesses big.

If you're a small business owner, you probably imagine that small companies are different and don't need branding as much as large companies do. Not true. The truth is small businesses need branding just as much, if not more, than large companies.

Perhaps you've thought about branding, but assumed you'd need millions of dollars to do it properly, or that branding is just the same thing as marketing. Nothing could be further from the truth.

Marketing is the engine of your company's success. Branding is the fuel in that engine.

In the old days, salespeople were a big part of the selling process. They recommended one product over another and laid out the reasons why it was better. Salespeople had credibility because they knew about all the products, and customers often took the advice they had to offer.

Today, consumers control the buying process. They shop in big box stores, super-sized supermarkets, and over the Internet — where there are no salespeople. Buyers now get online and gather information beforehand. They learn about all the products available and look to see if there really is any difference between them. Consumers also read reviews and check social media to see if both the company and the product are reputable. In other words, they want to know what the brand is all about.

The way of commerce used to be: "Nothing happens till something is sold." Today it's: "Nothing happens till something is branded!"

## DEFINING A BRAND

A brand is a proper name that stands for something. It lives in the consumer's mind, has positive or negative characteristics, and invokes a feeling or an image. In short, it's a person's perception of a product or a company.

When all goes well, consumers associate the same characteristics with a brand that the company talks about in its advertising, public relations, marketing and sales materials. Of course, when a product doesn't live up to what the company says about it, the brand gets a bad reputation. On the other hand, if a product or service over-delivers on the promises made, the brand can become a superstar.

# RECOGNIZING BRANDING AND ITS CHARACTERISTICS

Branding is the science and art of making something that isn't unique, unique. Branding in the marketplace is the same as branding on a ranch. On a ranch, ranchers use branding to differentiate their cattle from every other rancher's cattle (because all cattle look pretty much the same). In the marketplace, branding is what makes a product stand out in a crowd of similar products. The right branding gets you noticed, remembered and sold — or perhaps I should say bought, because today it is all about buying, not selling.

There are four main characteristics of branding that make it an integral part of the marketing and purchasing process.

## 1. Branding makes you trustworthy and known

Branding makes a product more special than other products. With branding, a normal, everyday product has a personality, and a first and last name, and people know who you are.

In today's marketplace, most products are, more or less, just like their competition. Toilet paper is toilet paper, milk is milk, and a grocery store by any other name is still a grocery store. However, branding takes a product and makes it unique. For example, high-quality drinking water is available from just about every tap in the Western world and it's free, but people pay good money for it when it comes in a bottle. Branding takes bottled water and makes Evian.

Furthermore, every aspect of your brand gives potential customers a feeling or comfort level that they associate with you. The more powerful and positive that feeling is, the more easily and more frequently they will want to do business with you and, indeed, will do business with you.

## 2. Branding differentiates you from others

Strong branding makes you better than your competition, and makes your product name memorable and easy to remember. Even if your product is absolutely the same as every other product like it, branding makes it special. Branding makes it the first product a consumer thinks about when deciding to make a purchase.

Branding also makes a product seem popular. Everyone knows about it, which implicitly says people like it. And, if people like it, it must be good.

## 3. Branding makes you worth more money

The stronger your branding is, the more likely people are willing to spend that little bit extra because they believe you, your product, your service, or your business are worth it. They may say they won't, but they will. They do it all the time.

For example, a one-pound box of Godiva chocolates costs about $40; the same weight of Hershey's Kisses costs about $4. The quality of the chocolate isn't ten times greater. The reason people buy Godiva is that the brand Godiva means "gift" whereas the brand Hershey means "snack". Gifts obviously cost more than snacks.

## 4. Branding pre-sells your product

In the buying age, people most often make the decision on which products to pick up before they walk into the store. The stronger the branding, the more likely people are to think in terms of your product rather than the product category. For example, people are as likely, maybe even more likely, to add Hellmann's to the shopping list as they are to write down simply mayo. The same is true for soda, ketchup, and many other products with successful, strong branding.

Plus, as soon as a shopper gets to the shelf, branding can provide a quick reminder of what products to grab in a few ways:

- An icon or logo
- A specific color
- An audio icon

# BRANDING IN A SMALL BUSINESS

Big companies spend millions of dollars on advertising, marketing, and public relations (PR) to build recognition of a new product name. They get their selling messages out to the public using television, radio, magazines, and the Internet. They can even throw money at damage control when necessary. The strategies for branding are the same in a small business, but the scale, costs, and a few of the tactics change.

### Make your brand name work harder

The name of a small business can mean everything in terms of branding. Your brand name needs to work harder for your business than you do. It's the first thing a prospective customer sees, and it is how they will remember you. A brand name has to be memorable when spoken, and focused in its meaning. If the name doesn't represent what consumers believe about a product and the company that makes it, then that brand will fail.

In building your product's reputation and image, less is often significantly more. Make sure the name you choose immediately gives a sense of what you do.

Large corporations have millions of dollars to take a meaningless brand name and make it stand for something. Small businesses don't, so use words that really mean something. Strive for something interesting and be right on point. You don't need to be boring.

Plumbers, for example, would do well setting themselves apart with names like "The On-Time Plumber" or "24/7 Plumbing". The same is true for electricians, IT providers, or even marketing consultants. Plenty of other types of business are so general in nature they just don't work hard enough in a business or product name.

## Even the playing field: The Net

The Internet has leveled the playing field for small businesses like nothing else. You can use the Internet in several ways to market your brand:

Website: Developing and maintaining a website is easier than ever. Anyone can find your business regardless of its size.

Social Media: Facebook and Twitter can promote your brand in a cost-effective manner.

# BUILDING YOUR BRAND WITH THE BRANDING LADDER

Even if you do everything perfectly the first time (and I don't know anyone who does), branding takes time. How much time isn't just up to you, but you can speed things along by understanding the different levels of branding, as well as the business and marketing strategies that can get you to the top.

## Introducing the Branding Ladder

Moving through the levels of branding is like climbing a ladder to the top of the marketplace. The Branding Ladder has five distinct rungs and, unlike stairs, you can't take them two at a time. You have to take them in order, and some businesses spend more time on each rung than others.

You can also think of the Branding Ladder in terms of a scale from zero to ten. Everyone starts at zero. If you properly climb the ladder, you can end up at 12 out of 10. The Branding Ladder below shows a special rung at the top of the ladder that can take your business over the top. The following section explains the Branding Ladder and how your small business can move up it.

| THE BRANDING LADDER | |
|---|---|
| **Brand Advocacy** | **12/10** |
| **Brand Insistence** | **10/10** |
| **Brand Preference** | **3/10** |
| **Brand Awareness** | **1/10** |
| **Brand Absence** | **0/10** |

# Rung 1: Living in the void

Your business, in fact every business, starts at the bottom rung, which is called brand absence, meaning you have no brand whatsoever except your own name. On a scale of one to ten, brand absence is, of course, zero. That's the worst place to live and obviously the most difficult entrepreneurially. The good news is that the only way is up.

Ninety-seven percent of businesses live on this rung of the Branding Ladder. They earn far less than they want to earn, far less than they should earn, and far less than they would earn if they did exactly the same work under a real brand.

# Rung 2: Achieving awareness

Brand awareness is a good first step up the ladder to the second rung. Actually, it's really good, especially because 97 percent of businesses never get there. You want people to be aware of you. When person A speaks to person B and says, "Have you heard of "The 24/7 Plumber?" You want the answer to be "yes".

On that scale of one to ten, however, brand awareness is only a one. It's better than nothing, but not that much better. Although people know of your brand, being aware doesn't mean that they are interested in buying it. Coca Cola drinkers know about Pepsi, but they don't drink it.

# Rung 3: Becoming the preferred brand

Getting to the third rung, brand preference, is definitely a real step up. This rung means that people prefer to use your product or service rather than that of your competition. They believe there is a real difference between you and others, and you're their first choice. This rung is a crucial branding stage for parity products, such as bottled water and breakfast cereals, not to mention plumbers, electricians, lawyers, and all the others. Brand preference is clearly better than brand awareness, but it's less than halfway up the ladder.

Car rental companies represent a perfect example of why brand preference may not be enough. When someone lands at an airport and needs to rent a car on the spot, he or she may go straight to the preferred rental counter. If that company has a car available, it's a sale. However, if all the cars for that company have been rented, the person will move to the next rental kiosk without much thought, because one rental car is just as good as another.

## Exerting Brand Preference needs to be easy and convenient

If all you have is brand preference, your business is on shaky ground and you can lose business for the feeblest of reasons. Very few people go to a second or third supermarket just to find their favorite brand of bottled water. Similarly, a shopper may prefer one store over another but, if both stores sell the same products, he or she will often go to the closest store even if it is not the better liked one. The reason for staying nearby does not need to be a dramatic one — the shopper may simply be tired, on a tight schedule, or not in the mood to travel.

## Rung 4: Making it you and only you

When your customers are so committed to your product or service that they won't accept a substitute, you have reached the fourth rung of the Branding Ladder. All companies strive to reach this place, called brand insistence.

Brand insistence means that someone's experience with a product in terms of performance, durability, customer service, and image has been sufficiently exceptional. As a result, the product has earned an incredible level of loyalty. If the product isn't available where the customer is, he or she will literally not buy something else. Rather, the person will look for the preferred product elsewhere. Can you imagine what a fabulous place this is for a company to be? Brand insistence is the best of the best, the perfect ten out of ten, the whole ball of wax.

## Apple is a perfect example of brand insistence

Apple users don't just think, they know in their heads and hearts, that anything made by Apple is technologically-advanced, user-friendly, and just all-around superior. Committed to everything Apple, Mac users won't even entertain the thought that a PC may have positive attributes.

Apple people love everything about their Macs, iPads, iPhones, the Mac stores and all those apps. When the company introduces a new product, many of its brand-insistent fans actually wait in line overnight to be one of the first to have it. Steve Jobs is one of their idols.

## Considering one big potential problem

Unfortunately, you can lose brand insistence much more quickly than you can achieve it. Brand-insistent customers have such high expectations that they can be disillusioned or disappointed by just one bad product experience. You also have to consistently reinforce the positives because insistence can fade over time. Even someone who has bought and re-bought a specific brand of car for the last 20 years can decide it's just time for a change. That's how fickle the world is.

At ten out of ten, brand insistence may seem like the top rung of the ladder, but it's not. One rung is actually better, and it involves getting your brand-insistent customers to keep polishing your brand for you.

## Rung 5: Getting customers to do the work for you

Brand advocacy is the highest rung on the ladder. It's better than ten out of ten because you have customers who are so happy with your product that they want everyone to know about it and use it. Think of them as uber-fans. Not only do they recommend you to friends and family, they also practically shout your praises from the rooftops, interrupt conversations among strangers to give their opinion, and tell everyone they meet how fantastic you are. Most companies can only aspire to this level of customer satisfaction. Apple is one of the few large corporations in recent history that has brand advocates all over the world.

- Brand advocacy does the following five extraordinary things for your company. Brand advocacy:

- Provides a level of visibility that you couldn't pay for if you tried. Brand advocates are so enthusiastic they talk about you all the time, and reach people in ways general media and public relations can't. You get great visibility because they make sure people actually listen.

- Delivers free advertising and public relations. Companies love the extra super-positive messaging, all for free.

- Affords a level of credibility that literally can't be bought. Brand advocates are more than just walking testimonials. They are living proof that you are the best.

- Provides pre-sold prospective customers. Advocate recommendations carry so much weight that they are worth much more than plain referrals. They deliver customers ready and committed to purchasing your product or service.

- Increases profits exponentially. Brand advocates are money-making machines for your business because they increase sales and decrease marketing costs.

For these reasons, brand advocacy is 12 out of 10!!

# BRANDING YOURSELF: HOW TO DO SO IN FOUR EASY WAYS

If you're interested in branding your product or company, you may not be sure where to begin. The good news: I'm here to help. You can brand in many ways, but here I pare it down to four ways to help you start:

## Branding by association

This way involves hanging out with and being seen with people who are very much higher than you in your particular niche.

## Branding by achievement

This way repurposes your previous achievements.

## Branding by testimonial

This way makes use of the testimonials that you receive but have likely never used.

## Branding by WOW

A WOW is the pleasantly unexpected, the equivalent of going the extra mile. The easiest and most certain way to WOW people is to tell them that you've written a book. To discover how you can write a book, go to www.BrandingSmallBusinessForDummies.com.

# Happiness:
# How to Experience
# the "Real Deals"

## MARCI SHIMOFF

I was 41 years old, stretched out on a lounge chair by my pool and reflecting on my life. I had achieved all that I thought I needed to be happy.

You see, when I was a child, I thought there would be five main things that would ensure that I'd be happy: a successful career helping people, a loving husband, a comfortable home, a great body, and a wonderful circle of friends. After years of study, hard work, and a few "lucky breaks," I finally had them all. (Okay, so my body didn't quite look like Halle Berry's—but four out of five isn't bad!) You think I'd have been on the top of the world.

But surprisingly I wasn't. I felt an emptiness inside that the outer successes of life couldn't fill. I was also afraid that if I lost any of those things, I might be miserable. Sadly, I knew I wasn't alone in feeling this way.

While happiness is the one thing we all truly want, so few people really experience the deep and lasting fulfillment that fills our soul. Why aren't we finding it?

Because, in the words of the old country western song, we're looking for happiness in "all the wrong places."

Looking around, I saw that the happiest people I knew weren't the most successful and famous. Some were married, some were single. Some had lots of money, and some didn't have a dime. Some of them even had health challenges. From where I stood, there seemed to be no rhyme or reason to what made people happy. The obvious question became: *Could a person actually be happy for no reason?*

I had to find out.

So I threw myself into the study of happiness. I interviewed scores of scientists, as well as 100 unconditionally happy people. (I call them the Happy 100.) I delved into the research from the burgeoning field of positive psychology, the study of the positive traits that enable people to enjoy meaningful, fulfilling, and happy lives.

What I found changed my life. To share this knowledge with others, I wrote a book called *Happy for No Reason: 7 Steps to Being Happy from the Inside Out*.

One day, as I sat down to compile my findings, all the pieces of the puzzle fell into place. I had a simple, but profound "a-ha"—there's a continuum of happiness:

**Unhappy:** We all know what this means: life seems flat. Some of the signs are anxiety, fatigue, feeling blue or low—your "garden-variety" unhappiness. This isn't the same as clinical depression, which is characterized by deep despair and hopelessness that dramatically interferes with your ability to live a normal life, and for which professional help is absolutely necessary.

**Happy for Bad Reason:** When people are unhappy, they often try to make themselves feel better by indulging in addictions or behaviors that may feel good in the moment but are ultimately detrimental. They seek the highs that come from drugs, alcohol, excessive sex, "retail therapy," compulsive gambling, over-eating, and too much television-watching, to name a few. This kind of "happiness" is hardly happiness at all. It is only a temporary way to numb or escape our unhappiness through fleeting experiences of pleasure.

**Happy for Good Reason:** This is what people usually mean by happiness: having good relationships with our family and friends, success in our careers, financial security, a nice house or car, or using our talents and strengths well. It's the pleasure we derive from having the healthy things in our lives that we want.

Don't get me wrong. I'm all for this kind of happiness! It's just that it's only half the story. Being Happy for Good Reason depends on the external conditions of our lives—these conditions change or are lost, our happiness usually goes too. Relying solely on this type of happiness is where a lot of our fear is stemming from these days. We're afraid the things we think we need to be happy may be slipping from our grasp.

Deep inside, I think we all know that life isn't meant to be about getting by, numbing our pain, or having everything "under control." True happiness doesn't come from merely collecting an assortment of happy experiences. At our core, we know there's something more than this.

There is. It's the next level on the happiness continuum—Happy for No Reason.

**Happy for No Reason:** This is true happiness—a state of peace and well-being that isn't dependent on external circumstances.

Happy for No Reason isn't elation, euphoria, mood spikes, or peak experiences that don't last. It doesn't mean grinning like a fool 24/7 or experiencing a superficial high. Happy for No Reason isn't an emotion. In fact, when you are Happy for No Reason, you can have *any* emotion—including sadness, fear, anger or hurt—but you still experience that underlying state of peace and well-being.

When you're Happy for No Reason, you *bring* happiness to your outer experiences rather than trying to *extract* happiness from them. You don't need to manipulate the world around you to try to make yourself happy. You live from happiness, rather than *for* happiness.

This is a revolutionary concept. Most of us focus on being Happy for Good Reason, stringing together as many happy experiences as we can, like beads in a necklace, to create a happy life. We have to spend a lot of time and energy trying to find just the right beads so we can have a "happy necklace".

Being Happy for No Reason, in our necklace analogy, is like having a happy string. No matter what beads we put on our necklace—good, bad or indifferent—our inner experience, which is the string that runs through them all, is happy, and creates a happy life.

Happy for No Reason is a state that's been spoken of in virtually all spiritual and religious traditions throughout history. The concept is universal. In Buddhism, it is called causeless joy; in Christianity, the kingdom of Heaven within; and in Judaism it is called *ashrei*, an inner sense of holiness and health. In Islam it is called *falah*, happiness and well-being; and in Hinduism it is called *ananda*, or pure bliss. Some traditions refer to it as an enlightened or awakened state.

So how can you be Happy for No Reason?

Science is verifying the way. Researchers in the field of positive psychology have found that we each have a "happiness set-point," that determines our level of happiness. No matter what happens, whether it's something as exhilarating as winning the lottery or as challenging as a horrible accident, most people eventually return to their original happiness level. Like your weight set-point, which keeps the scale hovering around the same number, your happiness set-point will remain the same **unless you make a concerted effort to change it.** In the same way you'd crank up the thermostat to get comfortable on a chilly day, you actually have the power to reprogram your happiness set-point to a higher level of peace and well-being. The secret lies in practicing the habits of happiness.

Some books and programs will tell you that you can simply decide to be happy. They say just make up your mind to be happy—and you will be.

I don't agree.

You can't just decide to be happy, any more than you can decide to be fit or to be a great piano virtuoso and expect instant mastery. You can, however, decide to take the necessary steps, like exercising or taking piano lessons—and by practicing those skills, you can get in shape or give recitals. In the same way, you can become Happy for No Reason through practicing the habits of happy people.

All of your habitual thoughts and behaviors in the past have created specific neural pathways in the wiring in your brain, like grooves in a record. When we think or behave a certain way over and over, the neural pathway is strengthened and the groove becomes deeper—the way a well-traveled route through a field eventually becomes a clear-cut path. Unhappy people tend to have more negative neural pathways. This is why you can't just ignore the realities of your brain's wiring and *decide* to be happy! To raise your level of happiness, you have to create new grooves.

Scientists used to think that once a person reached adulthood, the brain was fairly well "set in stone" and there wasn't much you could do to change it. But new research is revealing exciting information about the brain's neuroplasticity: when you think, feel and act in different ways, the brain changes and actually rewires itself. You aren't doomed to the same negative neural pathways for your whole life. Leading brain researcher Dr. Richard Davidson, of the University of Wisconsin says, "Based on what we know of the plasticity of the brain, we can think of things like happiness and compassion as skills that are no different from learning to play a musical instrument or tennis …. it is possible to train our brains to be happy."

While a few of the Happy 100 I interviewed were born happy, most of them learned to be happy by practicing habits that supported their happiness. That means wherever you are on the happiness continuum, it's entirely in your power to raise your happiness level.

In the course of my research, I uncovered 21 core happiness habits that anyone can use to become happier and stay that way. You can find all 21 happiness habits at www.HappyForNoReason.com

Here are a few tips to get you started:

1. **Incline Your Mind Toward Joy.** Have you noticed that your mind tends to register the negative events in your life more than the positive? If you get ten compliments in a day and one criticism, what do you remember? For most people, it's the criticism. Scientists call this our "negativity bias" — our primitive survival wiring that causes us to pay more attention to the negative than the positive. To reverse this bias, get into the daily habit of consciously registering the positive around you: the sun on your skin, the taste of a favorite food, a smile or kind word from a co-worker or friend. Once you notice something positive, take a moment to savor it deeply and feel it; make it more than just a mental observation. Spend 20 seconds soaking up the happiness you feel.

2. **Let Love Lead.** One way to power up your heart's flow is by sending loving kindness to your friends and family, as well as strangers you pass on the street. Next time you're waiting for the elevator at work, stuck in a line at the store or caught up in traffic, send a silent wish to the people you see for their happiness, well-being, and health. Simply wishing others well switches on the "pump" in your own heart that generates love and creates a strong current of happiness.

3. **Lighten Your Load.** To make a habit of letting go of worries and negative thoughts, start by letting go on the physical level. Cultural anthropologist Angeles Arrien recommends giving or throwing away 27 items a day for nine days. This deceptively simple practice will help you break attachments that no longer serve you.

4. **Make Your Cells Happy.** Your brain contains a veritable pharmacopeia of natural happiness-enhancing neurochemicals — endorphins, serotonin, oxytocin, and dopamine — just waiting to be released to every organ and cell in your body. The way that you eat, move, rest, and even your facial expression can shift the balance of your body's feel-good-chemicals, or "Joy Juice", in your favor. To dispense some extra Joy Juice — smile. Scientists have discovered that smiling decreases stress hormones and boosts happiness chemicals, which increase the body's T-cells, reduce pain, and enhance relaxation. You may not feel like it, but smiling — even artificially to begin with — starts the ball rolling and will turn into a real smile in short order.

5. **Hang with the Happy.** We catch the emotions of those around us just like we catch their colds — it's called emotional contagion. So it's important to make wise choices about the company you keep. Create appropriate boundaries with emotional bullies and "happiness vampires" who suck the life out of you. Develop your happiness "dream team" — a mastermind or support group you meet with regularly to keep you steady on the path of raising your happiness.

"Happily ever after" isn't just for fairytales or for only the lucky few. Imagine experiencing inner peace and well-being as the backdrop for everything else in your life. When you're Happy for No Reason, it's not that your life always looks perfect — it's that, however it looks, you'll still be happy!

By Marci Shimoff. Based on the New York Times bestseller *Happy for No Reason: 7 Steps to Being Happy from the Inside Out*, which offers a revolutionary approach to experiencing deep and lasting happiness. The woman's face of the *Chicken Soup for the Soul* series and a featured teacher in *The Secret*, Marci is an authority on success, happiness, and the law of attraction. To order *Happy for No Reason* and receive free bonus gifts, go to www.happyfornoreason.com/mybook.

# Break Down the Box

## Taking a Risk to Create an Amazing Life

### KIRK JAKESTA

Become who you were meant to be.

Listen to that voice in the back of your head that says, "I could do this."

Growing up as a young man, I quickly adapted to the lifestyle that was presented to me, a life that threatened to consume me, sending me into the dark path of life if I were to let it. Where the thought of change was not possible, not for me.

Perhaps you grew up in a lifestyle like mine where drug and alcohol abuse were the norm, where selling drugs as a young adolescent wasn't unusual but accepted, or you grew up in a good wholesome environment where life just made you comfortable with what you had. Deep down, we always want more. We want the best that life has to offer. In the back of our mind, our thoughts tell us that we are not worthy of it. We deal with the hand life dealt us and face the tough financial challenges without a leg to stand on, believing that we are not worthy of better.

Just getting by was my specialty, and still is. It was my normal growing up. My soon to be 75-year-old father is still working camp jobs as an excavator operator to this day, going in and out of retirement for the past 5 years, despite health limiting him from being able to see or hear properly. All this simply to make sure that he and my mother can have the basics. My mother is one of my best friends, next to my little love Aiyanna, who will turn 6 this year, and the love of my life, Amanda.

At 56, my mother suffers from rheumatoid arthritis and osteoporosis. Seeing your parents' heath deteriorate, especially after growing up thinking they were bullet proof, is a hard pill to swallow. My parents have been the best. They don't assume that they deserve much, so they don't reach for anything more, and honestly feel it's to late. That's where I want to step in. They gave me a good life. Despite growing up the way I did, my parents have been my crutch, and shaped me into the man I am today, along with the influence of my brothers and grandparents.

We all have close friends and family, whose aging has brought the reality of losing them closer to mind. Many of us have lost close family and friends to sudden loss. Tomorrow is never promised, and the best time to create a life worth living is NOW. My loved ones inspired me, and I want to inspire those who need it. To show that no matter where you are in life, there is always a fork in the road. If you are brave enough to look past the dark scary cover of it, then you will realize that life's greatest experiences are usually on the other side of fear. I want you to recognize that you deserve to tap into the greatness inside you! There is something more than the scraps of life. There is an amazing banquet, but if you don't respond to the invitation, then you will never be able to enjoy the feast.

The last year has brought some amazing opportunities my way, but first, I had to accept my invitation to the banquet. I had to take action and show up to reap the benefits. I'll admit, it took a major shift in my thinking, and it's a constant battle against procrastination, self-doubt and fear of failure. Even as I write this chapter, I realize that it took a lot to get to this point. I had to crawl out of that hole of self-pity, dust myself off and get back into the game. I needed to step beyond what I saw as possible in my everyday life, and instead believe that I had a greatness that could propel me forward if I was willing to take that leap of faith to create significant change.

Starting with my first self-development program and the potential for an amazing compensation plan, a seed was planted in me. I gained the mindset to be my own boss one day. To stop working 8-10 hours a day on another man's dream. When we think about how much free time we have, how much of it is wasted? Think about it; the average person sleeps 8 hours a day and works for 8 hours a day. That's 16 hours dedicated to sustaining a living and getting the proper sleep. There are 8 remaining hours that most of us aren't taking full advantage of. I know there are other essential activities that are accounted for in those 8 remaining hours, but you get the gist of it. I came to recognize that I could make my life extraordinary, but I NEEDED TO CHANGE MY MINDSET to tap into my ability. One of the hardest people you will ever have to battle is yourself.

Imagine stepping out on faith like that in your life. Having a vision for your future and then taking a leap without the proverbial safety net. My leap led me to many mentors; a self-development course through my now professional family, the Matrix group; an opportunity to begin exploring real estate investing by taking a few reputable courses; and of course, taking the leap and jumping into a book deal with an amazing powerhouse, world renowned speakers, authors, entrepreneurs, and now my co-authors, with the goal to pursue a speaking career to inspire First Nations people around the world. Note that all those opportunities gave back to me in a big way. They helped me to mentally prepare for the next opportunity, the next open door, and the next chapter in my journey towards an amazing life.

Each step I took led me to another networking opportunity, another inspiration, another mentor, and the momentum continues to build. I put myself on the path to find those "once in a lifetime" opportunities. Now I want to reach out to my people, becoming a role model and demonstrating that all things are possible. There is a life outside of your conditions, which is the reverse of the way you are living. It is possible to create a brighter future, but it starts with believing in yourself. Dedicate yourself to something, then great things will happen. You do not have to be a victim of your circumstances. Instead, you can take charge and be the change in your life.

You do not have to remain trapped by your ancestors' unfortunate past of residential school, and the horrible ripple effect of what they went through. For those who don't understand what they went through, that ripple effect has affected their children down through the generations in one way or the other. Now is the time to stop that ripple effect by making conscious choices in our lives to create change.

We must take responsibility for our past choices and actions, but more importantly, the ones we are making in the present. The present is all you can change, but the possibilities are endless if you are willing to move through the fear of the unknown and the fear of failure.

The point I want to make throughout this chapter is that you have the power to create, to build, and to change. It all starts with a willingness to open your mind to the possibilities and even to take risks to achieve what you have always dreamed of, even if you may have denied your ability to create that vision in the past.

I am here to tell you that all things are possible. You do not have to struggle through an endless loop of paychecks, overwhelming debt, and the hardship of not having the necessities. You do not have to let a troubled past get in the way of your amazing future. Instead, you can have a life that is rich in personal meaning and leaves a legacy behind for your children and grandchildren.

## CULTURE IS THE FOUNDATION FOR GROWTH

Our culture is one based on close-knit families and time-honored traditions. For hundreds of years, we lived in harmony with the land and each other. Time has changed things, and modern life does not seem to focus on this rich cultural heritage. I even find that the way I was raised limited my access to my culture, disconnecting me from what should be a greater part of my life, although I believe strongly that it is never too late to learn and make it a part of my family's life. I will continue to put forth the effort to make that happen even if it's with only little snippets throughout our lives.

What cultural heritage am I referring to? I am First Nations. I represent Nisga'a Nation, from the village of Gitlaxt'aamiks or New Aiyansh, and from my father's side. I am part of the Tahltan Nation. These are parts of who I am, although I truly wish the connection with these cultures was an even stronger part of my daily life. Still, it doesn't stop me from being who I am.

Why isn't it a greater part of my life? My childhood was not easy. I would say that I was undereducated, as the school system in my village was rated the second lowest in British Columbia. On top of that, we had a house built in the early 2000's. A few years after we moved in, we had a kitchen fire. It did a lot of smoke damage to the kitchen, leaving it completely charred. Nothing was done to fix it. That is a mindset that I grew up with, one where you learned to live with what you had. There wasn't an expectation that we deserved to have the kitchen fixed and, 15 years after the fire, that damage is still there. This is the reality of where I came from and who I am. So, you can see why I would want more out of life.

What about your own life? Can you see places where damage was done, but you did nothing to fix it? All of us deal with some type of psychological, physical, or emotional trauma. It could be a result of choices we made, or the actions of others that were not in our control. This world is a cruel place. In the end, however, it is up to you to decide if you want to live as a victim or be a victor instead.

Growing up with my two older brothers, I was confronted with circumstances that I could have blamed for my life choices. At home, there was a lot of fighting, drinking, and smoking weed. It was a tough environment for a young adolescent but that was my normal. Around 15 or 16 years old, I went from being a recreational marijuana smoker to dealing the herb. In fact, I became one of the biggest weed dealers in the community at one point. Then I moved to hustling harder drugs, to the point where I was making good money for a teenager. I didn't feel that great about myself or what I was doing to get that money. However, the lifestyle was so different from the years that my family struggled that it was hard to turn my back on the money.

That all changed the day that one of my friends offered herself to me as payment for drugs. It felt like an incredibly low point in my life. I started asking myself what I was doing. This was not who I was meant to be. I was completely shocked by her offer, and I couldn't accept it. I ended up giving her the drugs for nothing and quitting that business. I was done contributing to tearing down myself and others. Now I had to figure out how I was going to build myself back up and, in the process, how I could help others do the same. The answers were still a few years away, but I was at least on the track to finding them.

If I had not stopped then, I could have ended up in jail, dead, or with the death of someone else on my conscience. Your choices create your future. By making the choice to get out of that life, I changed my own future and I am grateful for it. I learned at a young age that life is truly about moments. Moments where you can either take the path less taken or the familiar one. Even though I didn't acknowledge it back then, I was making these life-changing decisions. I can see now that my conscience was in the right place.

That rough environment offered few opportunities for young people like me. As I got out of the drug world, I realized that I couldn't stay where I was. I needed to create an opportunity for myself. So, I headed to Vancouver, where I attended Vancouver Island University Trade School. I took classes to be an automotive service technician. After graduating, it became clear that this wasn't the future for me either. The men in the trade hated their jobs, and I realized I didn't want to be one of them. I was at peace with that. Even though I dedicated almost a year of my life to achieve that certification, I knew deep down I couldn't sacrifice my life to unfulfillment and regret.

I felt as if I was going through the process of elimination. The knowledge about what didn't work for me was as valuable as the knowledge about what did work for me. I started to understand myself better and believe that my happiness was mine to create.

# CREATING HAPPINESS STARTS WITH YOU

Happiness is not going to magically appear because of the things you own or the fact that you work 60 to 80 hours a week to bring home a paycheck. Instead, happiness is a state of mind, one that you can create, no matter your circumstances.

My determination to create change in my life led me to leave behind a life of drug dealing, and countless dead-end jobs. For the past 8 years, I have lived in Vancouver, where I started to do all kinds of different work, exploring my interests and trying to find my place in this world. I learned a lot about what I was good at, what I was okay at, and what I just struggled to accomplish.

During this time of exploration, I was still a typical young man, out to meet girls. They might not have been the girls that I could take home, but it was the life of a young man with few responsibilities. Then my daughter was born. She is my biggest inspiration, and I knew that I wanted to give her a better life than the one I had. Now I was inspired to do better, even if I wasn't sure how. I believed that if I did almost everything in the opposite way I was raised, I was going to be fine. In order to do that, I needed a new set of skills, and I needed a new way of thinking about the world and my place in it.

It was about becoming the role model that I wish I had when I was growing up, and finding inspiration in the young girl that now depended on me. To give her happiness, I had to be willing to claim it for myself to be able to provide a better life for her and my entire family. I'm a strong believer in "When I make it, we all make it."

Your happiness is a state of mind. You are in charge of your mind, not your circumstances. You can choose what to dwell on, and your point of view. I want to challenge you to recognize that you need to change your mindset about the circumstances themselves, thus creating happiness for yourself no matter where life currently has planted you.

# IS NEGATIVE THINKING HOLDING YOU BACK?

Some individuals seem to naturally be able to find the silver lining of any situation, and their joy in life is apparent. Even when they are faced with difficult circumstances, they focus on what they can learn and how they can grow, instead of becoming defeated. Granted, that does not come naturally to everyone. In fact, many of us are quick to fall into a negative way of thinking, one that keeps us focused on what has gone wrong and keeps us from acting decisively.

The reason I point this out is because if you want to achieve real change in your life, you need to be able to act decisively. A negative mindset will keep you from acting, simply because you will spend all your time talking yourself out of doing anything. The excuses can be numerous. Here are just a few:

- I don't have the money.

- I don't have the education.

- I don't have the skills.

- Those adventures are for other people. I have a family to take care of.

- The risk is just too great.

Negative thinking means that you tend to value the risk higher than the reward, so you freeze yourself in place, living with circumstances that you aren't excited about, simply because you can't accept the potential of risk.

Now if you aren't able to accept risk and you have a negative frame of mind, it can be very difficult to create the happiness you seek in your own life. It must start with a change to your own mindset, one that acknowledges risks but is not defined or held down by them. At the same time, I am not talking about a pie-in-the-sky type of thinking, the kind that cannot recognize challenges or potential issues.

Risk assessment is still a part of life, but the focus needs to be on how to mitigate the risk, not how to avoid acting so that you can avoid the risk altogether. When your mindset is in a positive frame, you are going to find that you look at risk differently. It is not an impasse or an obstacle that stops you from moving forward. Instead, you view it as something to be addressed, a challenge that can be navigated effectively. For every problem in life, there is a solution. The only thing that stops us is fear itself.

When you are focused on just surviving, and not on thriving, then no matter what soil you are planted in or the circumstances that you find yourself in, you are never going to be truly happy. In the quest for small moments of happiness, you are likely to make choices that are going to negatively impact yourself and those that you love.

Those choices could be anything, from drugs, alcohol, or even commitment issues. The point is that, long term, those choices are going to negatively impact your ability to make your situation better. Instead, you have now made your road even harder. Now you have another set of challenges to deal with, and those additional difficulties can be truly crushing to your mind and spirit.

Can you relate to some of these choices or ways of thinking? Can you understand negative thinking and using words like "can't," "won't," or "shouldn't" are keeping you from achieving what you were put on this earth to accomplish? As you can see, negative thinking can break down your spirit and leave you feeling as if you don't have the strength or ability to create change in your life. It can leave you feeling that your life is what it is, and you are better off just to accept it. I'm here to say f#!k that. Go Get Yours!

You are never truly stuck unless you choose to be. Can you find some light in the darkness, that inspiration and motivation you need to take the first step? I found it in my daughter, but it was also clear that I was changing my thinking and that was impacting my future in ways that I couldn't yet imagine.

## MANIFESTING YOUR NEW REALITY STARTS WITH YOU

During the time before my daughter was born, I had that moment all new fathers do, questioning the finances and trying to figure out how to pay for this new miracle in my life.

My answer was civil construction, which led me to eventually becoming a heavy equipment operator. I picked up the experience needed by jumping into a piece of equipment every chance I got. Straight up, I manifested that into reality. I had it in my mind when I first stepped foot in the field as a laborer, watching the guys run those big machines, that one day "that would be me."

Are there areas in your life where you need to be aggressive to achieve a goal? I could have sat back and waited for someone to give me an opportunity to learn how to operate those machines, but the truth is, that day might never have come. By seizing the reins, I created the opportunities for myself and achieved my goal. It wasn't easy, and I had to make some sacrifices. For two years, I worked the night shift. Starting out as the lowest paid laborer (which was still good money for a new soon-to-be father) and working myself up to be a lead hand. Delegating tasks and executing them in a safe timely matter. Here is where my life revolved around eating, sleeping, and going to work. I couldn't do anything else, and it wasn't the healthiest lifestyle. But it was also the first time that I manifested one of my goals, and it wasn't going to be my last.

In spite of all that negative thinking from my past, I decided to take a leap beyond what I had already accomplished. I decided that I didn't have to work to barely make ends meet for the rest of my life. I did have the ability to leave something for my daughter, and I had the power to create a legacy, one that would impact the generations to follow. The question was how?

## START WITH INSPIRATION AND ADD ACTION

No matter who you are and where you are in your life, there are individuals who inspire you. They are the ones who accomplish so much, despite the challenges and those who tell them that it can't be done. Yes, there are plenty of people out there who are going to tell you that nothing can change, you are risking too much, and that you will be sorry later. They might even claim that they are telling you these things for your own good, so that they can protect you.

That is not the kind of protection that you need. Instead, you need to be willing to take the risk, even be willing to fail. Fail forward. After all, if you never fail, then you will never know what it takes to succeed. You need to step beyond the opinions of others, beyond the fear, to have more, be more, and experience more.

To put it simply, failure is just a way of eliminating a process that wasn't going to work, thus allowing you to focus your time and energy on other options that might be more successful. At this point it is not a secret anymore. It's out in the open and has been for decades; failure is the crucial ingredient for success. You must treat each failure as part of the elimination process, one more step closer to achieving your goal. Eventually, something will give, and you will get the right idea or find the solution to your problem. This is a guaranteed result of dedicating your thoughts to your goal, and you best believe it works to the opposite effect as well. Your thoughts navigate your life. Whichever road you choose to go down is directly controlled by your own thoughts.

My goal was to achieve a better life for my family, and that meant figuring out what I was good at and what I wasn't good at. Simply choosing to abandon a course of action that isn't working can feel so liberating. Plus, every time you remove yourself from a course of action that isn't working, you are moving yourself closer to achieving your goals!

The inspiration for my next course change came as I realized that my mind was not fully in my work. I operate heavy machinery, which is not a job where you can afford to be distracted.

Instead, you need to stay focused on what you are doing and keeping the people around you safe as you complete the task at hand. Once I realized that I was in the place where I couldn't keep that level of focus, I knew I needed to take a break. It was my moment to take a leap and see where it would lead. I was inspired by several individuals, ones who took risks and were willing to give everything to make big changes in their lives.

Even though I am still working to this day after a bit of a hiatus, the skills that I picked up after all these years have given me the credibility to become a foreman after only two months coming back to the same line of work. That is a testament to the dedication that I once had to this specific line of work. Even though I know this won't be for the rest of my life, it feels good to know that I have what it takes to walk on to a new job, take control, and quickly establish myself in a key role.

What are you willing to give up? I bet you might be thinking that you aren't willing to give up much. Your life is comfortable, you have a routine, and even if it isn't everything that you hoped it would be, at least you understand the rules and expectations. That is where we all get tripped up from time to time. We choose the devil we know versus the devil we don't, because the unknown is scary. It is a dark hole and we don't know what might be hiding in there or lurking just around the corner. The truth is that what is lurking around the corner could be amazing, but too many times, we miss those opportunities because we are afraid to look.

Part of changing your mindset means accepting that taking leaps is critical to your success. The unknown is a place that allows you to grow and really craft your vision for your life. Fear is what keeps us in one place, holding onto things that might not benefit us, but are comforting because of their familiarity.

Think about it this way. If you know how to achieve a result using one process, you are likely to continue to use that process. However, if that process doesn't work as well as you like, you might explore other options and open yourself up to the idea of trying something different.

While that might work in the processes you complete at work, when it comes to taking greater risks in your professional and personal lives, there is a tendency to do the opposite. We tend to focus on dealing with the broken process, instead of trying to find an alternative and exploring other opportunities.

On the other hand, when I opened my mind up to the possibilities, I also unlocked my potential to create the life I had envisioned for myself. Therefore, be willing to be open to the possibilities. Do not lock yourself into one way of thinking, thus creating tunnel vision regarding what you are capable of accomplishing.

Even if the way that you are doing things has been successful in the past, you need to remember that life is not black and white. There is more than one way to skin a deer. What works successfully for one individual might not work as well for you. Don't be quick to lock yourself into one way of doing things, and thus be unwilling to consider other options.

Our world and society are geared to locking you into a position or a way of thinking, and then discourage you from taking the chance to make a change. Yet, those who have been the most successful, the ones who have created real shifts in how our world functions, started out by taking risks, breaking out of the expectations that had been put on them.

It is helping people create that change and break out of their expectations that inspired me to start a business with my partner, William, to assist aspiring entrepreneurs to be successful as they embark on the path of starting and building a business. At the same time, I have explored the possibilities of real estate investing, built a business using network marketing, and now have become a published author and one day a speaker that will inspire countless of First Nations people around the world. You can create that type of change in your life too! You just have to be willing to stop worrying about what people will think of you. Succeed or not, it's your life. Do what's best for YOU.

It involves breaking out of the box, taking a risk, and then reaping the rewards from stepping onto the path less traveled.

# UNDERSTANDING THE EXPECTATIONS THAT KEEP YOU LOCKED IN

A part of any society is the fact that expectations are built into how we are shaped. Cultures include specific events to mark our passage into adulthood. From our courtships through the building of our families, certain expectations are put into place for all of us, based on where we grow up and how we are raised. What can happen, however, is that those expectations can end up being roadblocks that keep us from moving forward and tapping our full potential.

In my childhood, there were multiple roadblocks; circumstances that could have kept me stuck on a path that left me feeling unfulfilled and unable to care for my daughter in a way that I wanted to. I could have continued the cycle of drug dealing and dysfunction, but I decided to strike out into the unknown. You have the power to do the same!

Therefore, I want you to think about the expectations that are part of your life. Are they serving you now or are they blocking you from moving forward? The biggest problem for my people is that the expectations are often set too low and our resources are often limited, and we are left with assumptions that we are not capable or worthy of more than a life of depression and struggles, filled with drug and alcohol abuse.

However, I know that there is more out there for all of us. It starts with a willingness to act on our own behalf, not waiting for someone else to do it for us. We must lose that sense of entitlement because nobody owes us anything. It's up to us to put forth the work that is needed to achieve what we want in life.

Every belief and value you have contributes to the decisions you make, and how you choose to act. Those beliefs and values can be altered as you experience different events throughout your life. Now you can choose to take those experiences and allow them to help you sift through those values and beliefs.

Do you regularly take the time to examine your values and beliefs? Do you ever ask yourself why you believe what you do, or why you value one thing over another? The reason it is important to do so is because you are going to make automatic decisions that impact your future based on those beliefs and values. Shouldn't they reflect who you are now instead of who you used to be?

Recognize that, whether you want to or not, you are constantly being exposed to influences that are changing and shaping you. How are you responding to this shaping? Many of us don't even consciously recognize how we are being altered by these forces, but once you are conscious of how these influences are impacting you, you can choose to accept or reject them. Take this for an example: McDonalds has their advertising everywhere. Literally globally. Everywhere you look, whether it's a billboard, on social media or television. Advertising for their new promotional meal or drink is constantly being programmed into your brain, so when you are hungry or thirsty you subconsciously have the thought of the new stuff instantly pop up in your head. This is all brainwash. The same goes for anything you allow into your brain, even a daily dose of inspiration. So be cautious of what you allow in and choose wisely.

Part of the importance of recognizing these influences is that many of them can keep you in a state of denial about the possibilities in your life. Others could be trying to keep you safe, so they discourage you from taking what they believe to be unnecessary chances. Still others are just negative in general and will tend to bring up everything that could go wrong, every potential obstacle, and even attack your intelligence for thinking about giving it a try.

Notice that those influencers in your circle are fundamentally trying to block you from taking a path that they may have decided not to walk themselves. They truly believe that if a course of action wasn't a fit for them, then it is not a fit for you. It is often the way that our communities, including family and close friends, try to keep us in their circle, but it also leaves many of us trapped in a life that does not benefit us, or allow us to fulfill our potential.

I am here to tell you that it is possible to create a life that you are excited about, one where you can take risks that bring you greater rewards. My life is altered, and I am excited about the future because I opened my mind to the possibilities beyond operating heavy machinery. Now, I am an example to my daughter about pursuing her dreams, regardless of where they take her.

As you shift your mindset, choosing to buck the beliefs of others, you are going to find that you repel those that continue to have a negative frame of mind and start to attract those with a positive and open mindset.

Throughout my journey, I have made decisions based on what inspires and motivates me, not on a fear that I need to get back to work. I am not counting the days until I need to report back to work or let them know that I am not coming back. Instead, I am enjoying this adventure. I am excited to see where it leads me because I know, even though I am not there yet, I am closer than when I first started.

You cannot let fears, especially those of a financial kind, keep you from taking leaps. So many of the inspirational individuals in our world took leaps without a financial safety net. They didn't have an emergency fund or a set date when they would no longer pursue a goal if they weren't successful. They believed in acting to achieve their goals, no matter what financial challenges came their way. An unshakable desire to success. They adapted WIT in their lives, which stands for "WHATEVER IT TAKES."

I want you to take on a mentality that allows you to focus on achieving your goals and overcoming the challenges involved. When you give everything to your efforts, you will see them come to fruition. It starts with recognizing that the people you surround yourself with are going to push you to try harder and go further, or they will focus on trying to pull you down and break your spirit.

## CREATE THE CIRCLE THAT SUPPORTS AND INSPIRES

The reason that I want to talk with you about the people you spend time with is that they are going to be part of those forces that influence you for good or bad. If you have specific goals that you want to achieve in life, then you need to surround yourself with those that will support you working to achieve those goals, while at the same time holding you accountable when you are working contrary to what you want to accomplish.

In the years since I moved to the mainland, I met someone who proved to be my biggest supporter and best friend, my dear love Amanda. As my significant other, she has the most influence in my world. If she had tried to stop me from pursuing my dreams, it might have meant the end of my journey. Instead, Amanda chose to step out in faith with me.

Without her, I do not believe I could have accomplished so much, so quickly. She stood by my side, took the leap with me, and our lives continue to blossom. She inspires me to never give up. I have found that surrounding myself with people who push me to be better and take chances are going to give me the fuel necessary to keep going, despite the challenges.

If you spend time with individuals that are not supportive, eventually you will give up. Your goals and dreams will remain unfulfilled and, years later, you will find yourself with regrets over what you should have done, instead of a sense of joy and accomplishment for what you have done. Remember, it is all about the influences that you allow in your life. Studies have shown that we become like the people that we spend the most time with. Who do you spend time with, and whose thoughts and ideas are you being exposed to on a regular basis? Do you have someone that you just know is in your corner that you are confident is adding value to your life?

It is easy to quit when you feel like you have no one in your corner. Amanda and I have been through many tough times, but the point is that we continue to stand together. You need to build that same type of support system, but also be willing to be that support system for others.

I want you to start focusing on how the people around you talk and act. Are they taking risks and inspiring others to follow their dreams? If not, you could be surrounding yourself with naysayers, those who are more likely to try to tear you down than build you up. If you want to make a change in your life, you need to first change your mindset, and then change who you spend your time with. After all, if you are changing your mindset, you need to spend time with individuals who will help you to reinforce that change.

Part of the way that I help myself to stay focused on a new open mindset is by choosing mentors that inspire me and give me critical food for thought. They help me to set my mind up for success. It is not about abandoning who I am, but recognizing that there is more to learn, to do, and more ways to grow as an individual who contributes to my culture and traditions. I also realized that they helped to set up my mindset to take even greater leaps and enjoy the opportunities that are available. It is not about the money, but about the fulfillment that comes from inspiring and being a role model for others from my community.

I choose to surround myself with mentors and associates that respect where I have come from, but who also challenge me to go further and to explore what the world has to offer. I want to leave a legacy for my family, but also to my people. I want them to recognize what is possible for ourselves and our nations. If you believe in yourself, you can achieve a lot in a short period of time, with or without a college education.

If you feel as if the darkness of life is overtaking you, I want you to stop and take an inventory of who you are surrounded by, and what type of encouragement they provide. You might find that they are taking light away and making the darkness appear that much worse.

The world is growing and changing constantly. We all have the wisdom born from our experiences, knowledge, and skills. Part of what makes us rich as human beings is the passing of that wisdom to others. When you find a mentor, you are finding a source of wisdom that you can tap into for your own benefit, and the benefit of those around you.

Start by looking for those that inspire you and then finding ways to interact with them. It could be through their writings or even their speeches. Use that inspiration to help motivate you to act. When you work with a mentor, you will find that you are pulled into their circle, and that will allow you to grow your circle with like-minded individuals who will help you to make the necessary changes to achieve your dreams.

I made some dramatic changes this past year, but much of that work started earlier. When I opened my mind to alternatives beyond the world I was living in, I started to believe I could act and create real change in my life. I saw the possibilities, and it was an exciting time. Still, I admit to having some fear and trepidation about whether I should actually move forward and take this leap into the unknown.

This is where your circle is so important. They will provide encouragement during those times of doubt, and when you wonder if you are truly capable of doing everything that you have ever imagined. Amanda provides that encouragement for me, and I like to think that I am just as supportive of her dreams. It is not a one-way street, but one built on mutual support.

Doubt is the enemy of those who want to build a different life, who see their purpose on a path that is not traditionally followed by those around them. You have the capacity to fight against that doubt by fueling yourself with positive thinking and gathering the tools you need to act.

What are some of those tools?

## THE TOOLS THAT CAN INSPIRE YOU TO CREATE

I have already spoken about how important it is to create a circle that supports, encourages, and holds you accountable to create real change. This includes finding mentors and inspiring figures. You do not have to feel limited to just one mentor at a time. Mentors can be part of all aspects of your life, both personal and professional.

Depending on what you want to achieve, you may look for a specific type of mentor who has already walked that path. Over time, you may find yourself choosing another mentor because you have achieved your first goal and are now focused on another aspect of what you want to achieve, which requires help from another individual with experience and skills in that area.

My mentors were chosen because what they said inspired me, motivated me, and gave me food for thought. Remember, my world experience was fairly limited before I started down this path of life. Yet, once I got started, it helped me to reassess my life and understand that nothing was truly out of reach. I just had to act.

Another important tool is to find a means to keep yourself centered on your goals and objectives. The world has a way of naturally distracting us from our goals and objectives, simply because we are presented with challenging circumstances that can appear out of our control. Therefore, it is important to find ways to allow your mind to quiet, thus giving you the opportunity to refocus.

There are a variety of ways to do this. I know some individuals find that peace and clarity when they take the time to exercise daily. Others prefer meditation, taking the time out of the morning and evening to clear their minds through breathing exercises or other forms of meditation. Still others prefer time in nature, where they can reconnect with the air, soil, and animals that are part of our home.

Whatever your preferred method, I want you to make it a regular part of your routine. You can focus on the vision of your achievements, giving them life and very clear details. The point is to make them as rich as possible to make them as real as possible. When you focus on visualizing yourself successful in achieving your goals and endeavors, you will empower yourself to create. You can see yourself acting in a way to reach those goals, which serves as the inspiration to keep you moving forward.

Athletes use visualization techniques all the time to achieve their goals. Doing so, those athletes are inspired to keep up the thoughts and actions that will allow them to do what they want and achieve their goals. They have created a mindset that gives them the ability to be successful, no matter what challenges might come their way.

I find that visualization helps me to manifest my dreams and goals into my reality. The richer the detail, the sharper the image, the faster I can make it happen. Discussing these ideas and dreams with my partner also helps me to see it clearly in my mind. Ask yourself questions to help you flesh out all the details.

Our ancestors often gathered for ceremonies that allowed them to make decisions which guided their course. It was early visualization, and I want you to tap into that. No matter where we are from or how we were raised, we all have the power to create inside of us. Our connection with each other and the earth is what allows us to find success, regardless of the challenges that come our way.

We all have encountered mental quicksand in our lives. It comes in many forms, but we need to be vigilant in looking out for it and avoiding it wherever possible. If you find that you have fallen into a quicksand trap, then you need to stop for a moment, allowing yourself time to reset your mindset back on the path you want to take.

Those resets are not easy, but they can be done with mindful and conscious effort. Do not be quick to assume that just because you were distracted or pulled into that mental quicksand that you cannot pull yourself up and move forward. The fact of the matter is that you will have moments where you fall, where you feel doubt, and where you wonder if you really can be successful. I want you to recognize that when those moments come, you need to walk through them.

It will not always be easy, but it is necessary that you make a conscious effort to do so. It will help you to grow stronger and also give you the endurance necessary to achieve anything you want in life.

When I took my leave of absence, I truly did not know what was going to happen next. However, I left myself open to whatever possibilities presented themselves. Essentially, you have to train yourself not to immediately say no, but be willing to say yes, no matter how crazy or ill-prepared you might feel for the situation. I had to open my mind to the possibilities and be open to exploring what the world had to offer, without fear.

I believe that what you want to achieve in life, you have the power to attract. The universe will give to you what you focus on. If you focus on the positive aspects of a situation and the possibilities available to you, you will draw more opportunities to yourself. A path you might never have embarked on will open up right in front of you. It is this power that you need to tap to create a real directional shift in where your life is headed.

One of the effects of creating change for yourself is that you end up being able to impact others. After all, you do not live in a vacuum. While others are influencing you, you are influencing others.

Think of how great speakers can get you to think differently, can inspire you to act differently, and can chart a different course for various institutions. I want you to recognize that you have the same power within you. We all do!

I want you to be inspired to see the valuable person that you are and use that vision to create and build a future that can be a guidepost to others. There are so many ways to impact others. Like a ripple in a pond, those efforts can spread farther than you ever imagined! Here are just a few of the ones that can give others a jolt of inspiration and leave you with joy and love in your heart.

**Volunteer** – Do you know how many organizations need volunteers to achieve their missions? You could work with young people, old people, people who have been dealt horrible circumstances, those struggling to overcome an addiction to drugs or alcohol, and so much more. You have the power to influence their lives for the better, just by your presence and a willingness to listen. Always remember that whatever inspires you, there is likely an organization trying to move that agenda forward. Take part and recognize the gift you give when you give of yourself!

**Invest** – I am not just talking about finding the right financial investments. I mean invest in people. Be kind, be willing to forgive, and be willing to lend a hand. When we invest in each other, then we can create large-scale change. Jesus Christ is credited with saying there is more happiness in giving than in receiving. Give to others and see how it benefits your mindset and inspires you to keep those investments going.

**Mentor** – I also want you to recognize that you can serve as a mentor to others. It is a gift that keeps on giving, one that can allow you to pass down your wisdom to others. Mentoring is not a top-down affair. Someone that you mentor can also inspire you as well. Be open to the possibilities and you can truly be a gift to another individual looking to create change in their life.

As you can see, my life is in motion right now. I am writing, investing, and creating the life that I want, one that will allow me to care for my family and pursue those items on my bucket list. I chose to move away from a dark path based on the past choices of myself and others to create one that is filled with light and laughter. You don't have to be chained down to a way of living that leaves with a lifetime of regrets. Instead, I want you to focus on what is possible and then make it a reality.

There is no vision that is too great or too small for you to achieve. The biggest obstacle that you will ever have in your life is the one that you create by means of your mindset. When you choose a positive mindset, you are blasting that obstacle out of the water. Do not see risk as something to avoid, but rather as a means to achieve even more in your life.

I want to inspire you and help you to move forward in creating dramatic change in your life. I am always available via social media, and for those who know me, feel free to see how we can work together, how I can serve as a mentor, or even just share with you what inspires me to get out of bed and keep my focus.

I hope that you recognize that the darkness in your life does not have to win. You can let in the light and achieve more than you might have dreamed was possible. For those that need a boost, see my story as one that you can create for yourself. Recognize that I am just getting started. Your willingness to pick up this book means that you are ready to take a leap, and are just looking for the motivation. I hope I have provided that! May the life you want be manifested in your reality, and may you tap into your creative abilities.

*"Use Your Struggles Today As Motivation For Tomorrow"*

— Kirk Jakesta

## Please visit Kirk Jakesta's website for more information, www.StreamLineToSuccess.com

# The Mindset of Success

## ANNA GRIFFIN

**M**y mother said something to me once that has stuck in my mind ever since, and that is, "Conviction and comfort don't live in the same block." If you want your life to be fulfilling and continually reach your goals and dreams, then there are going to be times of discomfort and overcoming fear.

When I started writing this chapter, I was completely filled with fear, uncertainty, and confusion. I guess it was fear of having my thoughts heard, and thinking, "Who am I to say all this?" or "What will others say?" These types of thoughts and questions often accompany us in moments when we least want it or expect it. "Am I strong enough?" "Am I going to be accepted and will I fit in?" are our common thoughts. But quickly enough I thought to myself, "Well, what's the worst thing that is going to happen?" I set myself back on track to have the right mindset and to think of the many exceptional leaders I have been fortunate to work for throughout my career and travels.

I've made it my mission to understand their exceptional attributes, which served them in moments of fear and self-doubt. But it is not always about the tools that are being used, the business models or the frameworks. Often, it is more about their mindset and leadership and what kind of people we become in their presence.

Living in many countries and getting to know different cultures, from the West to the East, I have had the privilege to better understand what makes a person successful, happy, and someone you would want to follow as a business leader, or because of their humble yet inspiring way of life.

So, I searched, and continue to search, for inspiration from them and the application of their mindsets, their extreme discipline, and their right habits in real life and workplace. The understanding of how we can be enemies to ourselves when it comes to fulfillment and achieving what we really desire in life prompted me to share and get it all out. Not only that, it was a true journey into myself that gave me clarity about what will come next.

In my book, Reimagine the Possible, I go into details of the attributes and tools of success and happiness, and how to apply them to your life. In this chapter, I am going to highlight some of them, to get you started on your road of possibilities.

# THE WILL TO CHANGE

*"It isn't the mountain ahead to climb that wears you down.*
*It's the pebbles in your shoes."*
- Muhammad Ali

There are a few distinct features that set successful people apart from those who fail. It's not always the talent or number of titles they have behind their name, but it's their mindset and the few things they do differently than majority of us. First, they are able to develop strong and fulfilling relationships, alliances, and connections that will help them build their business, create their success, and open the doors to potential opportunities.

Second, they don't procrastinate, but act on their plan, and the things they passionately want to do. Often, what most people do is wait until the perfect time comes and put things off till tomorrow that they should do today; e.g. "I'll start my new online business when I get more support from my partner or the economy is better," or "I will create a better website for my business once my kids get out of the house." "I will start taking care of myself later." There is always a 'but' that we keep saying to ourselves.

Third, they don't give up, they are persistent, and they keep going with their plan. They understand that success will not be achieved instantaneously. How often do we start something but never finish it because it gets too tough, too time-consuming, or too overwhelming? If we face those few things and persevere, I believe, we might be quite successful and happy in our professional and personal lives.

Of course, the journey is never easy. Success doesn't happen overnight. It will take time, but if you believe in your abilities, have the right mindset and perseverance, and above all work hard, you will get there. The hard work is not only related to achieving your professional or career goals. It is also hard work on yourself, your beliefs, fears, and habits, all of which this chapter will discuss.

What's important is not what you will or will not do, or whether you will or will not change. It is whether you have the will to change – to plan and act so that you can start doing the things that you know you should.

## NO SMOOTH MOUNTAIN

We keep dreaming about how one day we could reach our full potential, and the goals we always wanted to get to. But we often don't realize that we are as capable of genius as the most successful people in the world. We look at people like Oprah, Steve Jobs, and Richard Branson, and think, "If I only had their ideas, their genius", or "They are so lucky." You ask yourself, "How can I find my true purpose and passion in life? Why can't I never figure out how to be successful and happy like them?" But nobody, and especially the most successful in the world, thinks they are special until they make themselves special.

Nobody starts their business knowing that they will instantly become multi-billionaires. The difference starts with their mindset, the plan they have, and the actions they take. What sets the successful people apart from the less successful ones is that they do what most people don't want to do or are hesitant to do. Perhaps they hesitate because they are terrified of the unknown or they believe they are too busy, that it's beyond their capabilities, or maybe people around them would say it's not possible, that it is out of their reach and they will never get there. The other group, the fulfilled ones, listen to themselves and pursue their dreams, no matter the obstacles, and they ignore the naysayers.

Will you struggle? Will it be hard? Yes. You may fall many times, but who is counting? The best successes are made from failures. In fact, I don't believe there are failures, only lessons learned. You must remember that no single mountain is smooth. If you want to get to the top, there are sharp ridges that must be stepped over. There will be times that will be stressful, and you might be disappointed and discouraged.

# FEAR

*"No person can be confronted with a difficulty which has not the strength to meet and subdue. Every difficulty can be overcome if rightly dealt with. Anxiety is, therefore, unnecessary. The task which cannot be overcome ceases to be a difficulty and becomes impossibility and there's only one way of dealing with an impossibility, namely to submit to it."*
- Byways of Blessedness, James Allen

When we are confronted with difficulties, over time they create a great amount of anxiety. We may be faced with decisions that have long-term ramifications for our life or career and would affect not only us, but also those close to us. Those are decisions that we would rather not have to make. They just make us want to pull a blanket over our head and wish they would disappear together with the light that disappears once the same blanket covers our hair.

The question that I started to ask myself was, "Where are my fears coming from and why am I allowing them to stop me from moving forward?

James Allen's words in the quote are very profound, and the essence is that there is no problem that cannot be resolved. I like to think about it in this way: if an issue that I am facing can be resolved with an action, then I don't have an issue. It is simply something that needs to be resolved and is just something that we encounter in our lives or at work. So, remember, if an issue can be solved with action, then it is not an issue.

This has been my approach to any challenge that has been placed in front of me throughout my career and life. I treat it like something exciting to resolve and put my best effort into coming up with the best solution.

A substantial body of research shows that our brain can't actually differentiate physical fear (e.g. car crash) from emotional fear (e.g. being afraid of a spider). In addition, research also shows that in the brain fear and excitement are caused by the same neurochemical signals, i.e. cortisol and norepinephrine. Steven Kotler talks about this at length in his research, and shows that fear and flow (or the peak performance) are at the opposite sides of the same spectrum. They are both caused by the same neurochemical reaction in the brain, initiated by cortisol and norepinephrine.

Successful people learn to reframe the fear and use it as their compass; if something that they want to do produces some level of fear, then this is exactly what they will do. They will do what scares them the most, what feels uncomfortable. Only by doing this will they be able to push their boundaries, and this will give them the progress and growth needed to accomplish what they want. Below are some ways that help to acknowledge and reframe fear:

1. Acknowledge the changes that are happening and how they are affecting you – how does the event make you feel?

2. Ask 'Do I have enough information and facts to support my fear?'

3. Reframe the context. Say to yourself that you are excited about the event. This will switch your brain from feeling anxious and nervous to feeling excited and positive (no danger is coming).

4. What's the payoff? What is the price that I will pay if I don't reframe and stay in the state of fear, which will negatively impact my performance and future prospects? What will my career look like?

You must remember that we fear and are anxious about things that we create in our minds and imagine that they may happen to us. We think that external forces create our anxiety or fear and we only respond to those events. But our response to any situation, however bad it may be, is our choice and the result of our thoughts and beliefs.

I always like to remind myself that most things that we imagine out of fear never happen. Mark Twain famously once said, "I have lived a long life and had many fears, most of which never happened."

## MASTER THE MINDSET

"Beliefs have the power to create and power to destroy," as Tony Robbins, the motivational speaker and life coach, said. You see, our beliefs about the events around us or what happens to us are what shaped us into who we are today and who we will become tomorrow. But the fact is that many of us grew up around people who inadvertently passed on their limiting beliefs to us, and we might have been conditioned to the negative thinking that they grew up with. But remember, our past doesn't define us and there is no point in playing the blame game with them for passing their limiting beliefs onto you.

Research tells us that our thoughts and responses are shaped by our subconscious mind and they are aligned to the paradigms that we grew up with. For example, you might have had people in your life who constantly told you, "Since you haven't done it till now, you are just not cut out for it." This environment conditioned your thoughts and created paradigms in your subconscious mind. You start creating excuses without even realizing it, and eventually you will quit pursuing your dream.

If you want to have a successful career or follow your dreams, you need to evaluate whether your own mind is your biggest enemy and if you are acting according to old paradigms that shaped your thoughts, and hence your decisions, actions, and results. If so, a change is needed.

First, you will need to decide that you want to change your paradigm. Change is never easy, but once you realize that some of your old patterns, actions, and decisions are a result of the environment you were raised in or are surrounded by now, then you will see how this impacts your current life. I always like to remind myself of something that Wayne Dyer, American philosopher and author, said: "When you change the way you look at things, things that you look at change." Don't make yourself a victim of the circumstances surrounding you, or those that you cannot control.

Our life, career, and relationships are a reflection of the approach we take towards them. We are fully responsible for how things turn out for us – whether we are successful or not, have savings, a fulfilled relationship at home, a loving family, and so on. Let's say, your team is not producing the results you wish, or your business is not going well. Perhaps you are not paying attention to the relationships within your team and let them just run, or maybe the decisions you made were not the right ones. We are the only ones that have the power to take responsibility for the change we are looking for. We waste our most finite resource, time, to find external reasons that cause change. But once we shift this mindset, our life, career, and relationships will start getting into gear.

So, whatever we've learned and experienced in the past, we've accepted it as a truth at an unconscious level, and now it doesn't matter if what we've learned is correct or not, we still accept it as a truth. These are the 'life's apps' that we created for each aspect of our life – you have an app for everything that gives you a point of reference to go back to and check out how it should be done. I've realized over the years how this led to developing unconscious behaviors and habits in me.

*"The beliefs that you have about yourself and your abilities are not facts. They are your tightly held opinions. In other words, it's not primarily about your ability. It's what you believe about your ability that shapes your potential success."*
- Dr. Stan Beecham, Elite Minds

I also realized how often my belief system was empowering me or, unfortunately, disempowering me. You can take any experience in your life and make it into a very meaningful and empowering capability. Or it can be the opposite; your experiences and beliefs can be limiting you. You can take a painful experience and make it into powerful and motivating strength that will empower you to do anything you dreamt of.

There are a few simple ways that can help you work on your old paradigm and create change. I have done this myself, and it helped me realize how my own old conditioning was affecting my life, career, and relationships.

- Ask yourself: What are the same behaviors and actions that cause the same results and do not allow you to move forward?

- Think about successful people: What are the behaviors and actions they would take to get the results they want?

- Write down and focus on the new habits and actions that you want, and consciously think about them when you catch yourself doing the old ones.

- Change your 'I can't' or 'I should' to 'I must' and 'I will.'

# DON'T DRIFT...DISCIPLINE

For any muscle on our body to grow, it needs to be exercised and maintained continuously. The same holds the true for everything we want to accomplish at work or in life. If you want to be accomplished in anything, you need to get disciplined in doing things that matter, that are important, to bring you closer to success and set you on the path to whatever you want to do in life.

Of course, there are times when we need to take a balanced approach, but discipline for me is really an intrinsic quality that we all should strive for. It comes from within and starts with you. Oftentimes, we are looking for all sorts of shortcuts – the new meditation technique that will set us free, the new set of motivational tools, and the new supplement to get our body fit. But these may (or may not) work for a week, a month or 3 months, and if it's not coming from within us, it won't last. We don't do hard things if we are not emotionally attached to them.

If you look at leaders you admire, or the most successful people, you will see the level of discipline they have in their lives, and in doing things that set them apart from others, things that others are not willing to commit to. It is an intrinsic self-discipline – a matter of 'personal will' as Jocko Willink, a retired navy SEAL officer, calls it. The difference between being good and being exceptional is how disciplined you are.

He continues by saying, "Those who are at work before everyone else are considered best operators." But that discipline cascades down to everything else they do. Willink rightly said, in his book Extreme Ownership, that discipline equals freedom. This is very true – once you are disciplined with the things that you know you should be doing, it sets you free to do other things that you claimed not having time for, but which were in fact just an excuse, with the blame pointed everywhere else but at yourself.

# OWNERSHIP

One of the most important things I have learned, that really impacts how successful you will become, is to take full ownership of the results that you produce, the challenges, everything that impacts your results, or even your personal or social life. If I didn't own the results that were expected of me or my team to deliver, I would have never achieved the level and quality that I wanted. I always expect the highest results, but that can only be done if I completely own it. It is an attitude, and the fundamental block of any success. Blaming others or making excusing not only doesn't help but it actually hurts the team, the company, and ultimately you. In some cases, we don't want to even acknowledge the problem, or are afraid to accept that we made a mistake because we don't want to take ownership of the consequences. This will not serve the team or help it win.

Mistakes happen in the workplace, especially with complex problems, diverse teams, and tight deadlines. We should be able to acknowledge it, come up with better solutions for next time, or reach out to others for advice. We have much more respect for a person who takes full responsibility for their actions and results, don't we?

When we look at the great leaders and successful people around us, we wonder how they make the right decisions in stressful situations, or remain calm when faced with chaos and complexity. But what sets them apart in such situations is that they carefully choose how they respond. They don't jump to a conclusion and decide out of an emotional outbreak. This is a critical skill if you aspire to be a great leader and to be successful.

Often, what we do is react to situations without thinking, and we don't choose our behaviors but just act them out. We respond in the way our mind is wired and how we were conditioned. This may sometimes have catastrophic results in the workplace or in our personal lives.

Victor Frankl, the Austrian neurologist and psychiatrist, and a survivor of concentration camp, wrote a fascinating book "Man's Search for Meaning", in which he describes his horrific journey through Nazi concentration camps between 1942 and 1945, where he moved four times between different camps, including Auschwitz, while his family perished. Frankl said, "Between stimulus and response there is a space. In that space is our power to choose our response. In our response lies our growth and our freedom." This is a very profound thought that can guide us to make a shift in how we react and respond.

The best leaders and successful people train themselves and practice various scenarios for responding rather than reacting to the situation:

1. Think about consequences and bigger picture – What will you achieve by reacting in specific way (e.g. in anger)? Will the response and consequences be aligned with your goals or plans? How will the response best serve you, your family, or your project and company?

2. Realize whether you are responding or reacting – This is important, because it will give you clarity if you are reacting out of anger, a lack of control, sadness, jealousy or perfectionism. If you pause and think about the root cause of your answer or reaction, you will be able to respond in a wiser, more thoughtful way.

3. Don't react out of emotions – This relates to the point above, but you will also need to realize that your best response is based on facts.

4. Realize that you have a choice and different options – When you are faced with a situation where you want to rush to react and respond harshly, realize that you have a choice, and consider the consequences of your reaction. Count to three, if you must.

# HABITS

*"What we know from lab studies is that it's never too late to break a habit. Habits are malleable throughout your entire life. But we also know that the best way to change a habit is to understand its structure — that once you tell people about the cue and the reward and you force them to recognize what those factors are in a behavior, it becomes much, much easier to change."*
– Charles Duhigg 'Power of Habit'

A study was done by Wendy Wood, a Provost Professor of Psychology and Business at University of Southern California, on a group of people that was given stale popcorn in the cinema in exchange for rating a move. Most of the people ate the stale popcorn despite the fact that they said after the movie that they didn't like it. It turned out that they ate it out of their habit of being in the cinema. But what this shows us is that we often do things without realizing it and a, "Thoughtful intentional mind is easily derailed, and people tend to fall back on habitual behaviors," said Wood.

From the time you get up in the morning until you go to bed – most of what you do in between is without thinking; it's automatic. I mention automatic because it is a very important feature of habits, because we don't even realize what we are doing and why we do it. In fact, 40% to 45% of our daily activities is habitual, according to Professor Wood.

Everything we do or want to do is a step towards accomplishing a goal or achieving something that we desire – that goal might be to get to work, to satisfy hunger, to relax, to feel wanted, to get a promotion, and so on. Professor Wood explains that, "We find patterns of behavior that allow us to reach our goals. We repeat what works, and when actions are repeated in a stable context, we form associations between cues and responses."

It turns out that our brain creates patterns of activities, thinking, and behaviors that we do constantly and become automatic, so it doesn't have to spend energy to think about it each time (a simple example would be how to walk or brush your teeth). Our brain developed habits, so it doesn't have to think about them repeatedly and can have the space to focus on doing what's more important, like new projects at work, creating new product, writing, studying, making decisions, and more.

When we behave out of habit, our mental activity and alertness drops in the middle of it. Research shows that once we develop a habit and do something on autopilot, our brain is almost inactive, and so is our decision capability related to that activity. For example, when you are driving to work, you don't think, "Ok, now I need to decide to indicate that I want to turn right," do you? You don't make these decisions any more. When you were driving to work for the first time, you perhaps needed to think about which street to turn right onto. Over time, it became automatic.

Habits are developed slowly, and it is very hard for us to change the habit without completely knowing what the cues of that habit are. We must learn how to identify which cues led to a particular behavior, called cue awareness, so that we are at least aware and know when the habit is actually happening. Oftentimes, with certain strong behaviors, we don't realize the cue and, hence, we do them automatically. For example, some people bite their nails without realizing it, and they may now understand what the cue is (i.e. why they are doing it).

Have you found yourself with any habit that you do without understanding why, and you only realize it once you've done it? The important part of a change is to do it slowly through first recognizing when we have the urge or need to do the habit.

All successful people understand the importance of small improvements, which underpin our progress and have a profound impact on the long-term improvement. Imagine if you made just one tiny improvement every day. That small change, done every day, will turn into a habit and it will become part of your subconscious.

In the Japanese culture, this is called kaizen, which literally means 'improvement' or 'change for better,' and is fundamental to their professional lives and personal relationships. But the Japanese also understand that to see the change, we need to commit to it. Very often, what happens is that we set a goal, such as something that we want to improve. We might get excited and motivated at first, but that commitment fades after a few weeks and we forget to keep up our commitment. This comes back to understanding the triggers and wanting to change.

The single most important thing is our full commitment and then acting upon it. Without it, we will return to your original state in days. We really must be disciplined. At the end of the day, the most successful athletes didn't achieve their gold medals without true discipline. Yes, we will have obstacles, bad days, and days where we just can't do it anymore, but remember, after winter comes spring and summer. Don't think your winter will last forever.

Start small. Don't overwhelm yourself with too many things that you think you should, or want to, improve. It will only confuse you and you won't be able to achieve anything. To change your behavior long-term, you will need to:

1.  increase your performance little by little every day, and

2.  change your environment to get rid of the distractions that may keep you close to your old habits and behavior.

*"We are what we repeatedly do.*
*Excellence, then, is not an act, but a habit."*
- Aristotle

# GROWTH AND FAILURE

There are no happy accidents that turn people into experts or that give people some special gift which allows them to live a happy and successful life.

We are not born into it. While some could be genetic, most of it is not. When we are born, our potential is unknown. We can accomplish whatever we can possibly imagine, and our abilities can be developed.

When we read about successful people or observe those around us who seem to have more success than us, be it better jobs, better relationships, or better health, what they all actually have in common is their constant hunger for growth and development. They never stop learning new things and upskilling themselves, their mind is always curious, and they want to push the boundaries of what is possible. All these characteristics underpin their growth mindset, which is critical to their progression.

*"When you are in a fixed mindset, your success is a result of that belief. And all you will try to do throughout your life is to prove yourself against that fixed standard. In a growth mindset, challenges are exciting rather than threatening. So, rather than thinking, "Oh, I'm going to reveal my weaknesses," you say, "Wow, here is a chance to grow."*
- Dr. Carol Dweck

Growth mindset is a scientific theory suggesting that with effort, persistence, and hard work, our intelligence and abilities can be developed. Dr. Carol Dweck, a psychology professor for Stanford University, showed through over twenty years of study of human development and psychology that our belief system about our abilities and potential fuel our behavior and predict our success. Dr. Dweck's early research was focused on how kids respond to failure, and shows how some children reacted positively to failures and setbacks, taking them as opportunities to develop, while others were completely devastated by them. Those kids who thrived on challenges adopted a growth mindset. They believed that with hard work, good strategies, and perseverance, they would eventually develop more skills and talents. Those who wanted to stay away from failure at all costs were in the fixed mindset.

*"It's not how good you are. It's how good you want to be."*
- Paul Arden

Very often, we see people who have very fixed beliefs about their abilities, what can be done or achieved, and what they can accomplish in their career or in life. For example, you hear at work, "This cannot be possibly done," or "It's beyond my capabilities." Perhaps we may see that in ourselves at times. We may think, "I'm not good at this," instead of "What am I missing?"; "This is too hard," instead of "This may take some time and effort,"; or "I'm obviously not good at finance," instead of "I'm not good at finance yet and keep studying."

People who don't progress through their lives or career only see obstacles that prevent them from achieving what they want, or what is achievable at all. They look at their abilities, skills, and performance, or even their health, fitness, and relationships as fixed and accept them as they are. This "fixed mindset," as Dr. Dweck describes, "makes us believe that our character, intelligence, and creative ability are static and cannot change or improve in any meaningful way."

You may see multiple examples of a fixed mindset around you. There might have been several projects or initiatives that were believed to not be achievable or were too hard to implement, and hence were abandoned. A project manager believed that the timeline was too short; there were no right skills or resources within the team; no right leadership or systems to support it; and the reasons why not could go on forever. Focusing on issues rather than solutions, and the things that would prevent the team from being successful would, indeed, bring no results.

With the right mindset and approach, even hard tasks can be achieved, issues can be resolved, and step by step, you will take the team closer to success. Remember that if an issue can be resolved with actionable tasks, you actually don't have an issue. This requires the right mindset to be in place, one that will see unlimited potential and the bending of the boundaries of what's possible.

This is what successful people do. If we look at the people whose success we admire, then we will see that they cultivate their growth mindset to enable their personal, professional, and social development and progression. Research shows that one of the reasons why we feel unhappy or frustrated in our jobs or personal lives is that we stop growing and progressing. We, as humans, are "designed" to evolve, and progress and growth is necessary to our wellbeing.

*"If you imagine less, you will be what you undoubtedly deserve."*
- Debbie Millman

With the growth mindset, as Dr. Dweck explains, we treat any setback as an integral part of our development and path to success. I have felt bad, embarrassed, or fearful of my mistakes and setbacks, but I've learnt that they would only help me to grow. Often, I came out on the short end with my decisions, but every time I aimed to tweak my approach to do better next time.

Growth mindset keeps our mind sharp. In today's work environment, we need to keep up with new technological and organizational developments. Things are changing and won't slow down anytime soon. To be ahead, we need to constantly learn.

Sometimes we find ourselves in moments where our fixed mindset kicks in, but the important thing is to realize it, snap out of that, consider more appropriate approach and move forward. Through "deliberate practice" we can change it – we must be purposeful and systematic about what we want to change. What helps me shift when I find myself in a fixed state are the four simple steps outlined below. They require a focused attention, and once you go through them, you will realize how destroying and limiting your fixed mindset can be, and instead will focus on developing more of a growth one.

1.  Be aware that you are exposed to limiting thoughts based on your past and learn to be aware of your fixed mindset thoughts. What I mean by that is that we are prone to reject new opportunities, not because we are not able to do it, but because we are afraid of the unknown. Our brain is wired to search past experiences and do only what is known and in our comfort zone. Remember that this is only your brain's response to the unknown. It wants to keep you safe and it doesn't like risks and any unpredictability.

2.  Acknowledge that you have the choice. We all have a choice about how we react and respond to any situation. How you interpret challenges, setbacks, and criticism is your choice. Whether you apply a fixed or growth mindset, it will have a chain reaction in what will happen next.

3.  Replace fixed mindset talk with a growth mindset voice. Personally, I have had many moments when I dealt with self-doubt and feared to take on new challenging projects, was simply procrastinating, or too

lazy to do something. We have all been there. Over the years, though, I have learned to replace those damaging thoughts of a fixed mindset with the empowering thoughts and beliefs for growth. When I doubted myself and thought, "Can I do this? This is certainly not for me. I don't have the talent to do this," I immediately replaced those thoughts with empowering thoughts, such as, "I am certain I can do this and I will learn along the way," "I have passion and perseverance to accomplish this."

4.  Take action that focuses on growth. Without action, there is no progress. Without facing the challenges and new opportunities, you will never learn. You must wholeheartedly commit to the challenge and overcoming any setbacks that will come your way. Learn from it and adjust as necessary.

## FAILURES ARE YOUR GIFT

It is no secret that our worst fear is a fear of failure. However, failure is actually a good thing. It is just an opportunity to begin again, learn from it, and to do it more wisely next time. Encouraging our fears and failures prompts the most necessary changes in our lives and businesses. This may be true, but we don't often feel or think like that.

When we make mistakes, we feel terrible and disappointed; we lose confidence, and get discouraged. We just don't want to continue or go through it again. What we are actually doing is missing out on the primary benefit of failure. Winston Churchill once said, "Success is the ability to go from one failure to another without losing your enthusiasm." The man was right.

When it comes to failures, our egos are our own worst enemies.  When something is going wrong, we try to save face and our defence mechanisms kick in, and we often find ourselves in denial. It seems very hard for us to admit and to try to learn from failure, because it requires us to challenge our status quo.

*"I haven't failed. I have just found 10,000 ways that won't work."*
- Thomas Edison

Look at Walt Disney, who was fired from the local newspaper he worked for because he was told he had no imagination. What his story teaches us is that just because you encounter a setback or end up on another path, it doesn't mean that you are stuck. Keep learning from your mistakes, apply changes to make things better, and you will get back on track eventually, and most likely, you will be better off than before.

There are many successful people who we can mention here who have failed but never gave up, e.g. Steve Jobs, Oprah, JK Rowling. What separates successful people from those who are unsuccessful is that they have a huge amount of perseverance. They never give up or let their failures define them. They pick themselves up even stronger than before and keep going. It's not always easy to continue moving forward, but when you keep pushing onwards, despite the failures and obstacles along the way, you are already ahead of all those people that just gave up. I find that the secret really is to just show up and try your best over and over again.

Failures are part of the process. To be successful, you must learn how to make it a tool rather than a roadblock. You must be adaptable and agile. When you stop learning from your mistakes, then you will stop growing and developing. You should take any failure as motivation in pursuit of your dreams. Don't let it stop you but grow you instead. The only failure there can be is when you quit. Learn the lessons, apply them, and you will come out stronger than before. You will never learn faster than you will by executing something.

## NOTHING HAPPENS WITHOUT ACTION

Remember, talk is cheap! Action is everything. Our thoughts are catalysts to get started. But our thoughts are not things, and nothing will happen without taking those thoughts and putting them into action mode. That's what successful people focus on. They know that talking, planning, and analysing won't get them too far. It's their actions that will trigger all the things on their road to success. To be successful in any part of your life, you must be action-oriented. Mark Twain said, "The secret to getting ahead is getting started." You can't do everything at once, but you can take it step by step. Incremental changes every day will work in the long run.

Try to keep the momentum to get you closer to where you want to be. You can develop a plan to work on your habits and then pick one to focus on at the time. Commit to it!

## BANNISTER EFFECT

One of my favourite stories, which I would like to finish off with and which I personally find very inspiring, is the story called The Bannister Effect. In moments of doubt or thinking that something is not possible, I always return to it and remind myself that what I might believe is not possible can actually be achieved. Before 1954, it was believed that running one mile under 4 minutes was physically impossible, that the human body could not possibly do it. In 1954, Roger Bannister, an English middle-distance athlete, ran it in 3.59 minutes, breaking what was believed to be an impossible record. But what happened next is remarkable – once it was known that the mile could be run in under 4 minutes, many other athletes accomplished it, and with even better results.

What this shows us is that it was not a sudden leap in the evolution of the human body that broke the physical barriers. It was a shift in thinking. Bannister truly believed that it was possible to run faster and break the record. He visualised himself achieving it over and over, and his mind accepted it as reality. The story also shows us that once we see that something can be done, something that was once believed to be outside of our realm of possibilities, we can also achieve it.

In our daily work or life, our mindset has the ability to limit us or set us up to achieve the impossible, not only for us but those around us, our team, our peers, and our family. We are in control of whether we will conform to what is socially accepted or try to believe beyond it. If Bannister believed that the record was 4 minutes, and nothing could be done about it, that it was a physical limitation, then he would never have been able to break it. He would never even have tried to do it.

Just like this story, what often keeps us from achieving what we truly want is the barriers that only exist in our mind.

## To connect with Anna Griffin please visit
## www.ReimagineThePossible.com

# Power, Purpose and Passion

## TONY DAVIS

Many people struggle in the maze that's the rat race of life. They feel like they're missing some vital clue that would release them from the endless corners and dead-end stretches. They might not enjoy their work, or they may be putting in too many hours of their time or there may not be enough dollars left over at the end of each month. Life often seems complicated and difficult to balance. Yet, when I ask people what they wanted to be when they grew up, the answer is typically a job (a doctor, fireman, architect, etc.). Why is this? Why should your job define who you are as a person? Why is the answer not to be a good person? Or, a great husband? Or, to be in love? We all have gifts and talents that we can use to be impactful in both work and life. So why do only a minority of people ever reach their full potential? The answer is quite simple. They fail to utilize the gifts and talents I just mentioned. In fact, it's often the first place people go wrong when creating their self-definition. It's a misalignment that can easily complicate and disorder life. On the other hand, when you're able to form a connection between what you love, your gifts, talents and purpose, not only will you be put on a path towards a more prosperous career, but it will also be a significant one—a life you love and of which you're proud. This chapter will show you how to make this connection by aligning your power, purpose and passion for leading a more fulfilling and successful life.

## THE CORE

To avoid falling into the trap of defining yourself by the wrong things (and the problems associated with doing so), you need to find what's at your core. However, it's challenging to make it through this maze without knowing your end goal. Money and work are essential parts of life's puzzle, but they aren't the only things that matter. Your dreams and your passions are also pieces. In life, you'll often set a goal and see this as an ideal. You'll choose a college major, for example. You'll then work to finish it, get a job in that field and, after a while, what you had felt was ideal might start feeling like an ordeal. In this type of situation, it's common to start looking for a new deal. The problem with this is when you constantly move from deal to deal it's hard to make wealth because you typically leave something behind each time you move. However, when you build on top of something else, you can generally go a lot further. If you truly know what's at your core, then your end goals will be aligned with who you are, and it will be less likely for you to drift into an ordeal. Throughout what follows, we'll build a framework so you can find what is at your core and keep your real deal, ideal. Finally, don't think it's too late to start; just start.

## DEFINING YOUR END GOALS AND FINDING YOUR PURPOSE

The Cheshire Cat from *Alice in Wonderland* captures the idea of travelling without knowing your endpoint, when he says, "If you don't know where you are going, any road will get you there." One of the fundamental things to succeed in life is to know where you're going. The need to know where you are is equally necessary because, without your bearings, it's impossible to formulate a plan to arrive at your destination. Thus, the key is knowing both what you want and what you have. To help develop this path—navigating from where you are to where you need to go—a diagram has been included below.

**How Power, Purpose, Passion and Principles Interact**

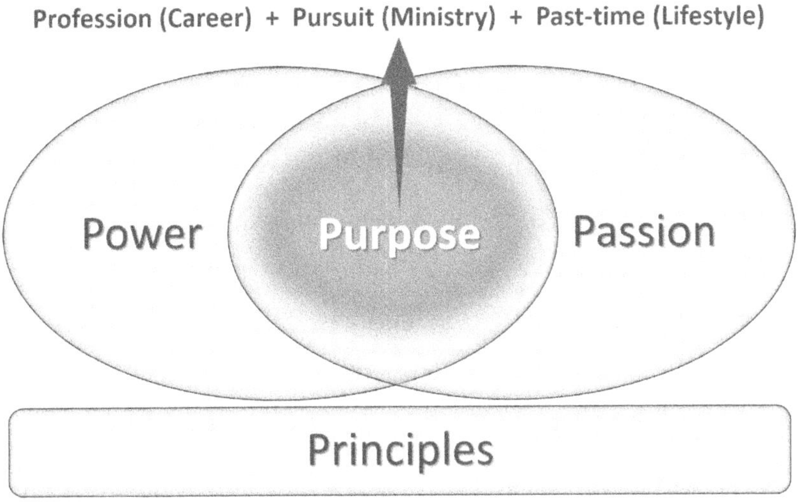
Profession (Career) + Pursuit (Ministry) + Past-time (Lifestyle)
Power
Purpose
Passion
Principles

# THE ROAD MAP TO YOUR PURPOSE: COMBINING POWER AND PASSION WITH PRINCIPLES

The above diagram acts as a concept map, where the different aspects of your life originate. These puzzle pieces of life generally fall into two essential circles, your Power and your Passion. Together they form the foundation of the diagram, with their intersection being its centre and most important part. This intersection is where your purpose is found. It represents all your end goals. Your actions and decisions in life should always guide you towards it, helping you find a path that allows you to flourish in life and be happy. But to understand it, we must now look at its components.

**Power**

The first section we'll consider is the circle in the diagram labelled "power." Power represents your strengths. Your strengths can fall into one of two different categories. The first category is your natural strengths, which are the talents and traits you're born with. The second category is your learned strengths, which are the skills you get from experience and education. This is where many people go wrong. They end up relying primarily on their learned strengths over their natural strengths. They get trapped doing what they've learned to be good at but do not necessarily enjoy or have been "wired" to be good at. They rely too much on past education—the courses they've been sent on and what their lives have led them to do—rather than what they were naturally born to do.

Those in this situation feel that they have invested too much time already and that they have too little time left to change focus to their natural strengths. They fear that if they attempt to change, they'll lose the time and work they've already invested. However, they fail to realize that by not adapting to encompass their natural strengths, they live life on a lower level and may never achieve the heights they could naturally attain. This is a painful lesson to look back on in your later years.

What's critical is to build on what you truly have, your natural strengths and learned strengths. It allows you to improve by maximizing the time you've invested already while laying the best foundation to optimize the future. When people align their work with their natural strengths, their work doesn't feel like such an ordeal; instead, it becomes something to look forward to each day because it's easy—it comes naturally. Aligning your work in such a way can be difficult without conscious thought, as these strengths are not always self-apparent. Often natural talents are things you probably don't even know you have, or don't know are special. They are things you may do without thinking and traits you might assume everybody has, but may actually be uncommon. Ask those closest to you, "What am I good at?" Ask yourself, "What do others ask me to do? What do they seek my advice on?" These often reveal your natural strengths, especially the ones you take for granted.

## Passion

This moves us onto the second circle in the diagram, which is labelled "passion." Passion represents the things that you love doing. You spend at least eight hours a day at work, which is a third of your day, and over time this will add up to nearly a third of your life. You should be doing what you love at work because it represents such a large portion of your life. If you don't, you'll spend a significant amount of time doing something you dislike, and it will wear you down and drain your energy. Why, then, are so many people part of the "Thank God it's Friday" club? What will these people do at the end of the month? Will it be "Thank God the month is over? … the year is over? … my life is over?" Would it not be better to be part of the "Thank God it's Monday" club? It's possible to wake up in the morning and be excited—if you love what you're doing. Not only does working for something you're passionate about make you happier, but it also allows you to contribute more to your work. When you enjoy something, you can work at it longer and harder. It fuels you to stay the course through stressful and challenging times. You can get things done even when it doesn't seem possible because, despite the task being hard, you still enjoy what you're doing. This will lead you to get more done over time and, additionally, your enthusiasm will show in your work and make it of better quality. It now becomes easy to see how working in your passion can not only complement your power but also improve upon it.

## Purpose

Where power and passion overlap, you find your purpose in life. When you can connect your power with your passion, you're performing at your peak potential. In other words, when you love doing something and you're good at it, it will come easy, and the results will be excellent. You'll get the feeling that time just flies and others will seek you out, be it at work or in your private life. The more you develop this, the better you'll become and the more you'll be paid! If you aren't regularly feeling this at work, you need to re-evaluate what you're doing. Even if you had enjoyed it at one point, this is a sign that your ideal may be becoming an ordeal. This sign alone doesn't mean the work you're doing is wrong for you or, by extension, that your ideal is misaligned. What it does mean is that something needs to change. Sometimes, it means you've slipped out of purpose and are focusing just on learned strength and money (the rat race). Sometimes you're still in your purpose, but you've forgotten why you're doing it and just need to reframe and find what made you passionate in the first place. Remember that life is simple: when you're strong at something and passionate about something, you're on purpose. It's important to realize that when you aren't on purpose, you won't enjoy life or what you're doing. You may enjoy it for a short while, but it won't last. Something will be missing.

## Principles

Before unpacking more on purpose, you need to understand something critical: principles. You can't fully define your purpose without knowing your principles. Without principles, it's impossible to be successful. In the preceding diagram, your principles underlie the whole picture. Your principles are the core values that are important to you: your beliefs, your code of honour your priorities, etc. If your life and work aren't aligned with them, nothing else will matter. This is because when you break one of your core principles, you can't win. You'll self-sabotage before you can get anywhere. For example, if you (secretly) believe that it's wrong to make money or that rich people are bad, when a great business opportunity comes around that would make you a substantial profit, you'll subconsciously let the deal fall apart. You won't even know why it failed, but it will be your self-sabotage that stopped it from being successful. Going against your core values will only set you back, and even if you do manage some success, you won't be happy because the guilt of going against your principles will seep into your life. What's exciting, though, is once you understand your principles and get everything properly aligned, your life will explode through your purpose. When you understand your principles, you can use them to guide all your decisions—it makes life so simple and easy! Put these things together and life will really start to happen for you. Your principles and your purpose will always align, as both your power and passion are fundamentally entwined with your values. Once you have achieved this, your life and work are going to feel natural and everything will come together. Use your principles to navigate your passions and your power and decisions will become easy. You'll have a more fulfilling life and will find yourself living in your purpose.

## UNDERSTANDING YOUR PURPOSE

Purpose has three aspects to it, which we will unpack in this next section. These are:

1. Your profession, which is everything to do with your job, career, investments; what you do to make money.

2. Your pursuit, which is everything to do with your significance in life, your ministry, charity, "give-back" and legacy; how you impact the world without making money from it.

3. Your pastime has everything to do with your lifestyle, hobbies, friends and fun; it's what you do that you enjoy but from which you don't make money.

These three aspects of purpose are more clearly revealed when we add a third circle (profit) to the first diagram, as shown below. It also explains how we get out of purpose, and the effects of that digression.

### How Profit Influences your Purpose

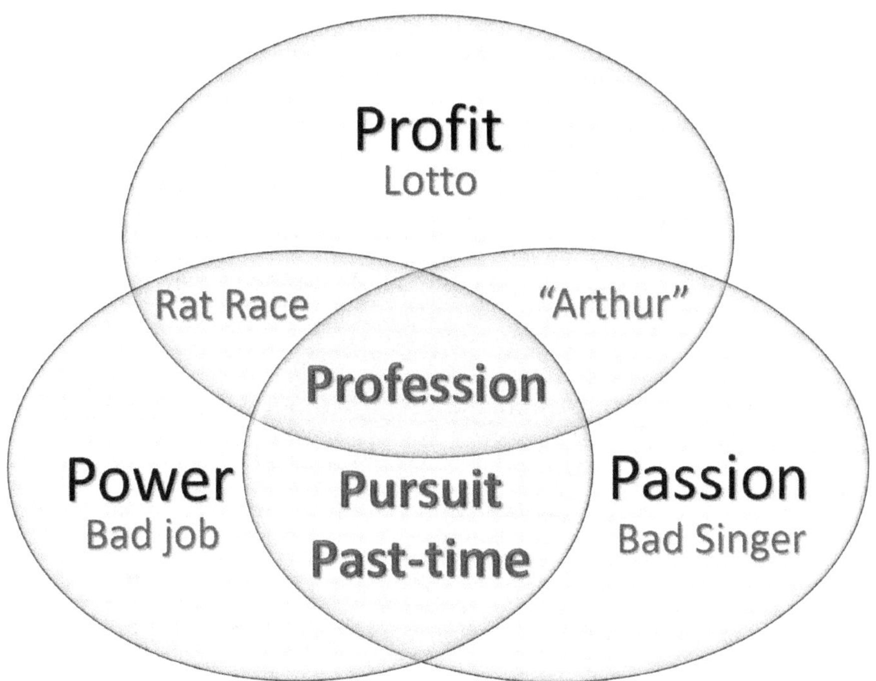


The profit circle sits much like power and passion, having its own space but also intersecting the other circles and making new quadrants. You can be in profit but not in power or passion. However, your goals and actions should always move you towards the centre of the diagram and into your purpose. Understanding the categories outside of your purpose will help you evaluate your situation and move you towards actually being in your purpose. Let's first look at these sections that are outside the central purpose section (represented by Career, Ministry and Lifestyle).

If you're only in your passion, you may enjoy something but aren't good at it, nor are you profiting. It's like being a bad karaoke singer—you love it, but no one else does! People tend only to do things in this section when they're trying out a new idea, hobby, instrument, etc. They usually aren't making money as they aren't good at it. So, it doesn't become a career and, typically, they don't stick it out as they aren't good at it.

You can also have money but no skills or passion. This is like being the lottery winner and is rare indeed! One must remember, though, a fool and his money are easily parted. So, this will also likely not last. If you're lucky enough to find yourself here, you better learn some money management fast!

Now, if you combine passion and profit without skill, you get the film character Arthur, the trust fund kid who loves his life but does nothing. This will also not last, as there's no meaning in that life. It's also a rare place on the diagram for someone to fall.

A more common area is when someone's good at something but not passionate about it, nor making money from it (or really poor money, perhaps). This is the bad job where you're working near minimum wage just to scrape by, even though you may be good at it. This is a fairly common quadrant, and there are millions of people around the world who live here as a means of survival. However, in most first world countries, people tend to move out of this quadrant as they realize it is a bad deal. They do so by moving to a new deal or by learning and improving their skills to get better at what they're doing and, thus, attract better payment.

When people find themselves in the quadrant of just profit and power but no (or little) passion, it's called the rat race, and this is where the vast majority of the population falls. This is the "Thank God it's Friday club" where people are working outside of their passion and are just chasing money. While people can earn a lot of money in the rat race, it's not a good place to be. These are the people who are always complaining or have midlife crises as their life is meaningless and miserable. They are the ones who go and buy a new car or boat to try and bring themselves happiness or meaning. Many people slip into the rat race without intending to. They start with something they love and are good at but end up chasing the money and building a career they don't enjoy but get well paid for. They become rich in money but poor in joy. Of course, this doesn't imply that all rich people are miserable. Not at all. The contented rich have excellent lives because they're working in their purpose.

## THE THREE TYPES OF PURPOSE

When power, passion and profit combine, it creates the central quadrant known as career— or profession or prosperity—because it isn't just about the money, it's about excelling at what you love at work. Money is not the most important thing, but it's of considered importance with power and passion. It's a balance, which brings great joy and prosperity and makes the most significant impact in the world of work. Money is necessary because you can do a lot with it. You can use it to ensure security and stability for your family. You can also use it like great philanthropists, to do good in the world and improve other people's situations.

When you are working in your passion, on something you love, time flies at work. You also increase your abilities at a much faster rate. It's surprising how few people do this! Perhaps it's a throwback from school where students are told to work on their weaknesses so they can pass the exams. Life becomes a never-ending slog to improve what you're bad at doing. This doesn't work. You hate it, and you never get really good at it. If you work on your weaknesses (at work) the best you can become is mediocre. Companies and clients don't pay for mediocre. But if you work at what you love and what you're good at, you get better and better and become excellent. People pay a lot for excellence. Don't slip into the rat race; adjust your direction and get back into your purpose-focused profession. That's where you'll really earn, but you need to choose that direction. Your boss won't do it for you.

However, this still leaves us with one blank space in the diagram and the other sub-region of purpose. It's what happens when you link your power and passion but without profit (money). Some may ask if this is something to strive for. Is it also part of my purpose? Most definitely! The blank space I'm talking about is just as valuable as the profession section—it's just that most people don't consider it because it doesn't involve their "day job" and making money. It contains the following two sections.

## Pursuit

Pursuit (or ministry) encompasses all the things you want to do in life (that are within your power and passion), and that you want to do to help other people. Think concepts like ministry, legacy, significance, and giving back. An excellent example of someone who lived their life in this section was Mother Theresa. She was good at what she did and she loved it. It was a life-work for her but it did not make her rich. Although this type of life is not for everyone, you must still have some things in your life that fall under pursuit. These can be all sorts of things, and they don't have to encompass all your time or be "world-changing." They can even be small, and seemingly insignificant. They just need to be what you can do to improve the world around you. It's what you do for others to return the good fortune you get from being in your purpose. This brings a tremendous amount of happiness and meaning to your life and makes a difference to those around you.

**Pastime**

The second section here is called pastime (lifestyle) and encompasses your life outside of money and significance. It includes things you love to do (and are good at) that make life worthwhile. Think of things like family and friends, hobbies, and lifestyle. For example, you could be a great parent or spouse, an excellent host and entertainer. You may have a hobby you love, like being good at gardening or painting and not make money from it. This is fine because of the enjoyment it brings you and those around you. And yes, these are part of your purpose too. Imagine thinking that being a great parent was not part of your purpose!

## PERSONAL MISSION AND PERSONAL BRAND

Finally, your purpose will express itself in two ways: internally, it will be expressed as your personal mission and, externally, as your personal brand.

Your personal mission is what drives you and guides you through life and work. It will help you define the path you need to succeed. Your personal mission tells you what's important to you and will be formed out of your principles (your goals, priorities, beliefs and values). It will motivate you and will be the map to getting you where you need to be. For example, Oprah Winfrey is well known to all. Her personal mission has driven all she does. She is true to it and as a result she has grown a multi-billion-dollar business (brand). Her mission? "To be a teacher. And to be known for inspiring my students to be more than they thought they could be." She writes that, when she started, "I never imagined it would be on TV."

On the other hand, your personal brand will be how you manifest your purpose to those around you – how they see you. You will use this to communicate to others why you're doing what you are doing. It will also be how you use your purpose to sell yourself and the products or services you create. In turn, your personal brand will be essential to profiting from your purpose. Remember that this is what others see and they'll respond accordingly. Once again let's look at Oprah. Her outward brand is huge: TV personality, retail, advice etc. As one of the most recognized brands in the world, when she puts her name on something it transforms it into an overnight success. It's huge—but it wasn't always so. However, she stuck to her personal mission and created her own brand by being faithful to her way of living out her mission (challenging millions of viewers to live their best lives possible by understanding their own potential) even when others opposed her or said it wouldn't work. Sir Richard Branson has done the same.

Both are very important. Without your mission, it will be hard to get to where you need to be, and it will be easy to become misaligned with your passion and principles. Without your personal brand, it will be hard to be able to develop your power and, without that, it will be hard to make money or impact the world around you.

## HOW DO YOU GET TO YOUR PURPOSE?

Now that you know where you need to be, you must now find how to get there. Andy Stanley said, "It is your direction not your intention that determines your destination." This is the principle of the path. Let's say you wanted to drive from New York to Miami. If your car is on the highway to San Francisco, it doesn't matter that you intend to go to Miami, you won't end up there. You're on the wrong path, going in the wrong direction, and it's your direction that will determine your destination, not your intention (what you want). Once you realize you're on the wrong road, it doesn't help to change your car, or to fill up with petrol or drive faster. None of these things change your direction. While these types of changes don't make sense in this example, many people still try similarly stupid sorts of changes in their life all the time. They try working harder or get a second job, but make no progress going towards where they want to go.

To get where you want to be, you first need clarity or to understand your intended destination. This is your purpose and your personal mission in each of the three different areas. Once you know where to go, the beautiful thing about direction is that you can change it in an instant. Furthermore, your ability to change direction means your past doesn't determine your future. Obviously the past does have an influence because it has brought you to where you are now. However, your past does not dictate or decide your future path. You really can choose where you want to be. You must, of course, realize that just because you change direction doesn't mean things will improve instantly—you won't just "arrive" at your intended destination. Just as if you had driven twenty hours towards San Francisco and then corrected your path to go to Miami, you'd still need to make up that time. But at least you're now headed towards Miami!

In changing your direction to your life purpose, you'll be on the right path, and one step closer to where you want to be every day. You're never too old to get where you want to be in life. Nothing will change if you keep moving in the same, wrong direction. The first step of getting anywhere is to decide not to stay where you are, then decide to change, then take action. If you make that decision now you can get almost anywhere in the next five years. That's infinitely better than a lifetime of regret and what-ifs.

## MAKING IT HAPPEN

We all end up somewhere. Those who end up where they want to be do so on purpose. Everything worthwhile that exists begins with a purpose (personal mission) followed by a carefully crafted plan that is driven with massive action and the determination to succeed.

Many people don't understand their purpose, and that's where they fail because they don't get around to defining it. They have no clarity and live their life in doubt and confusion. Then there are people who understand their purpose, but it's just a daydream. They have no action plan or haven't decided to change direction and implement the plan. To make your purpose a reality takes not only a plan but also much work to execute. When implementing change, you'll always be challenged, and you'll need the determination to see it through and not quit along the way.

We must live our lives on purpose, as in the end, we only regret the things we did not do. A year from now, you'll wish you had started today. Don't put things off. Instead, say "I'm glad I did start today." In five years from now, do you want to be in the same place you are now? Or do you want to be at your intended destination? You can be. Start the change today, and live your life in your chosen future. Live on purpose!

## To contact Tony Davis or find out more about how to live your life on purpose, email him at purpose@adavise.com

# Think in Solutions – Your Way to Success

## ASTRID SCHMITT-BYLANDT

**H**ow easy is it to say "this is not possible", or "I can't do this", or even worse, "you can't do this"? Then we move on and don't give the issues a second thought. I have these situations in my office every day and every time I challenge my colleagues by asking, "Imagine I wasn't here – what would you do?" Miraculously, everyone can always come up with a solution.

Don't get me wrong. That solution might not always be the one that we go with or one that works, but unless you change your thought process and your mindset, there will be many things that you are able to achieve but don't, because you are not even trying! When you feel like saying "I don't know how" or "that's not possible", make a point to always come up with at least ONE solution. Start today.

Different ways of changing thought processes work for different people. Make a list, write down all solutions you can come up with, even the funny, the weird and the "impossible" ones. Even the silly ones. Discuss the issue with someone you don't know that well to get a different perspective.

One of my friends challenged me the other day and asked me, "How about we do some magic and conjure up a perfect partner, boss or staff?" Yes, I know, magic has not exactly been perfected yet. However, by brainstorming and writing down all your thoughts, you can develop your list and start working towards your solutions. Once you start this habit you will come up with a variety of suggestions that you might not have initially thought about. Step by step, you will develop new thought processes.

So many people come up with the things that are "not possible" as it is so easy to focus on the negative. Make TODAY the day you stop this habit! Let today be the start of Thinking in Solutions!

In my office, I have five key points that everyone has to learn for growth and success:

1.  Assumption is the mother of all f**k-ups.

2.  Take responsibility for all your actions.

3.  Be persistent – always chase and follow up.

4.  Always connect with new people and continue building your network.

5.  Think in Solutions!

The first four could fill a whole book but I will only go through them briefly in this chapter. However, the last point is a real passion of mine. People that have taken my training and/or in my employment that understand this, progress is exponential. It is phenomenal to watch their improvement and development every single time. (For more in-depth details, please visit my website at www.solutions-finder.com, see how I can help you find your solution.)

Last year, one of my colleagues told me that a specific castle and garden in England was not allowing groups for sightseeing. I asked for the phone number and spoke to the person in charge. Let's call him Jim. We chatted for a few minutes and then I told Jim about our client who really wanted to see the castle and gardens. I told Jim that our client was coming from abroad and would there be any way this group's visit could be made possible within the set of restrictions of the castle.

I simply asked if this could be made possible. I worked around HIS and his company's needs, and I tried to find common ground. He said ok but only in the afternoons and the group could not have their own guide. They would need to go through as individuals. That was ok with the group and EVERYONE was happy. I offered to pre-pay for the entrance fees immediately and when it came to booking again this year, Jim was happy to take another two groups the same way. Despite initially being told it was not possible, I was able to work out a deal that worked for everyone.

## Think: What can I do for you? What would work for you? How can I help you?

A few years ago, I helped one of my friends who produces high quality rain and greywater harvesting solutions for airports, housing and other big building projects, to get an appointment with a specific engineer, who seemed to be blocking my friend's systems for all of his construction projects. My friend found it impossible to get hold of this particular engineer. Again, I asked for the phone number, I picked up the phone, asked for the engineer, got him on the phone, and arranged a time for a meeting with my friend. Now you might think, everyone can get lucky. Of course! However, this barrier my friend had in his head regarding the engineer being hard to get hold of didn't exist for me. I picked up the phone as if to call my mum or my friends. In my mind, there was no issue. I had no negative thoughts on this. In fact, I had no thoughts other than wanting to schedule a meeting. Had the engineer not been in the office, I would have asked his colleague for a time to call back. If the engineer had still not picked up, I would have asked to have a meeting or phone conversation scheduled. If you really want something, then persistence is one way to bring solutions.

## Think: Be results driven and never give up!

For me, the word 'no' from someone else just doesn't resonate unless I have tried myself.  Of course, it's not always possible to get someone to say 'yes'. You might say, "I can't go over my boss's head" or "I can't constantly do other people's work if they don't achieve what they should". No, I am not saying you should. You also have to cut your losses and think about what your time is worth to YOU. Perhaps your time is spent better achieving something else. Are there other ways or other things that you should be doing instead? Just because I can spend a lot of time on achieving something that others tell me is not possible doesn't mean I should necessarily do it.

However, it is crucial that, in order to start thinking in solutions, you change your thought process. Ask yourself if anyone famous you can think of could achieve what you want to achieve and might get a 'yes' in a situation that you feel is 'impossible'. If the answer is "yes," then your focus needs to be:

- How do you think they would do it?

- How can I or we make it possible?

- What does it need?

- Who could I ask for help?

- What solutions can I or we think of?

Money, I hear you say, is what makes most things happen. And yes, you are right. If you have a lot of money, you can employ more people. It's easier to ask people for favors and you might have a bigger network of people with skills, talents and contacts. Yes, money makes it easier, but that doesn't mean that things are otherwise impossible!

Solutions come in a variety of forms. Brainstorming is just one way. Always keep in mind: different people equal different views. Talk to your work team as well as the few key people that are part of your inner circle. Speak to the people from your sports groups or any of the groups that you might belong to. Ignore your habit of thinking that the issue might be difficult or impossible. Start fresh, every time! If your mind is focused on solutions, creating new ways and thinking about new routes and methods will become second nature. You'll surprise yourself with what you can actually achieve in life, in love and in work.

## Think: If you need new inspiration, change your surroundings.

Change the people that you speak to about your issues. Change the environment you are sitting in or working in, or even where and how you sit. Change your lunch or dinner routines. Change your route to work or your gym routine. Give yourself a chance to gain different perspectives. Start meeting new people. Start networking with different people from different professional and social circles. Start new evening courses, read new books, find new things to do in your spare time. Nothing should keep you from finding the solutions that will lead you towards your path of success.

## START WITH YOUR ROUTINES AND YOUR LANGUAGE

Often, we don't even notice when something has become a routine or a habit. Our minds do it on autopilot. We may get to our destination without having a conscious memory of the events that got us there. Even when there's a shift in our routine, it can be hard to break habits and we might find ourselves continuing to follow the same path because it's convenient or easier.

A few weeks ago, my normal route to work was blocked. I had to take a detour. Even on day two, three and four, I forgot that my "normal" route was closed. For days, I drove around the corner of my house right into the "road ahead closed" sign. I am sure we have all been in that situation before. We do something every day and it becomes a this-is-how-it's-meant-to-be way.

Actively find other ways and always know that you have the power to act.

Your daily routines often dictate your reality. Stop for a moment and think about what you did yesterday. Make one small change TODAY.

I can already hear the excuses about why it is not possible to change your life:

- But I can't...

- But how?

- But my kids, husband, family, boss, friends, etc.

- But I don't know...

- But I don't have the money…

- But I don't have time…

## STOP!

Start with the mindset of searching for your solutions. Finish with the mindset that is focused on the obstacles. Time and money are something we can all make if it is important enough!

**Think: Stop your routines – replace them with new ways.**

# DAILY LIFE SCENARIOS THAT CRY OUT FOR NEW SOLUTIONS

These are a few typical scenarios I see in my coaching sessions. Within a short chapter I can, of course, only scratch the surface of how things can be worked on and tackled. But here are a few examples:

### Relationships

If your relationship is on the brink of failure, start by asking yourself:

1. What does my partner want from this relationship? (yes, start with your partner and not with yourself!)

2. What do I want from this relationship?

3. How can we successfully move forward setting goals and breaking them down into small steps?

4. What is the measurement to know when I have achieved step one?

5.  What can I do to take the next step?

Then set steps two, three and four - one at a time.

Implement each small step immediately and start the change now! Remember, though, it might well be that what the other side wants is just not what you want. Sometimes, it is time to move on. However, without starting to find common solutions, you will continue in the same rut, day in, day out.

## Moving house

You want a new house? Then go out and find it! Define what it is that you want, where you want to live, how you want to live - SEE where and how you want to live! Visualize! Paint a picture or cut out the kind of housing that you can see yourself living in from ads or magazines. Go to the areas you want to live in, check the schools, the bars, the sports clubs or whatever it is you are looking for. Analyze your situation and determine what your options are. Do you have enough money for a deposit? Can you re-mortgage your current home? Can you sell your home and then move? Can you borrow money? Can you make extra money by taking in a lodger for a period of time to build up your savings? Can you move to a different area which is cheaper or closer to work or your children's school? Can you save money by doing or not doing things? Can you rent out a room to a language school and take in a student for a few months each year? Can you rent out a room on Airbnb? Tackle the "what" and "where" first and then tackle the financial side exactly the same way. But again, you need to start and take action NOW.

I won't go into the financial side as many books have been published about this and one paragraph will not do it justice. However, I would like to mention this sudden realization from one of my staff. I'll call her Rita:

Rita: "I just bought my lunch. I bought one of the plastic bags to carry the stuff back to the office. The bag costs GBP 0.10, which is not that much. But, if I went shopping three times a week and had started shopping at 10 years old, by the time I turned 90 I would have spent GBP1,248 in plastic shopping bags!!! That's two holidays for me!!"

## New job needed

Unhappy with your job? Then find a new one! Easier said than done, some of you will say. Whatever the reasons you might have for not changing there is a solution! Focus on the positive even if you have been unemployed! What skills do you have? What makes you happy all day, every day? What do you really want to work in? What new qualifications might you need? How can you get them? Who can you ask to help you prepare your CV or prepare you for interviews? Who can you ask who might know someone in the field you would like to go into? What do you love doing? Who does what you do or want to do? Find that person who is successful at what you would like to do! See if you can work with or for them. If necessary, offer to work for free for a week or more to show that you are the right person for the job. If that is not possible, try and work on a few weekends or in the evenings. Find five or ten potential ways and explore all of them to find your perfect solution. Adjust your outcomes each time to move in the right direction.

Decide:

1.  What is it that I actually want?

2.  What and how does that look like and feel like?

3.  What do I believe is holding me back?

4.  How can I solve the issues that I believe are holding me back?

5.    What is the timeframe I want this change to happen in?

6.    Who can I ask for help?

Start researching your new job options. Start scheduling those interviews. Plan for what you are looking for. Are you a part-time mum interested in a part-time job? Or, do you want a bit more income as a pensioner or perhaps the multi-million-pound new job! Focus on what you want and work on finding the right solution every day.

Every new step has to be planned and you have to start TODAY! Just like learning how to walk, take a baby step each day. Only you can take these steps. No one will do it for you.

Actively change your ways. Get those different perspectives. Shake up your routine by trying something new or different. You can't reap the benefits of change without shifting your mindset and perceptions. You have to find the right solutions for yourself.

**Think: Action, even in the form of a small step, is a step in the right direction!**

# THE ADVANTAGE OF COACHING

Remember when your parents, siblings or teachers said, "Do you want to learn how to walk, talk? Play the piano? Play tennis, football, etc.?" Each day you improved a little bit by following a step by step process. Today, you can swim, play tennis, speak a language, or whatever you started learning in your earlier years.

If, today, you had someone who said, "I know how to do what you want to achieve. I'll take you by the hand and walk with you, come what may," wouldn't you immediately say, "YES. Please show me!"

FIND that person who has done what you want to do.

FIND that person who will listen to what you want to achieve, who can teach you what you would like to learn and hold you responsible when you slack. Be proactive and persistent in looking for the solutions that are right for YOU.

## Think and write down: What do I want to achieve and what are all the ways I can think of to start me on my journey to success?

Unfortunately, as children, we don't always appreciate free education. However, as an adult, education can be expensive. All too often, we wish we had learnt languages, math, etc. at school, studied harder or been taught X-Y-Z subject, for example, business, media, making/managing money, setting up your own business, etc. There is no back to the future time machine yet but you can move forward! It is never too late to start afresh with anything you would like to have and enjoy!

My mum found love after my dad died when she was 74. She turned 92 this August and what an amazing 18 years they have already shared and hopefully, they will have many more years to come of travelling, going out and appreciating each other's company. Remember, it is never too late!

If you are ready to learn, then you can find online courses, free YouTube tutorials, sports classes, evening classes and, of course, mentors and coaches. I have helped many people through their life's crises over the years. It took a long time to fully realize that this is a skill that I hugely enjoy. I have supported many people move forward in life and achieve their goals. Now I finally made this into my perfect job. I started looking at patterns in what I was doing, and

I started thinking about how to use this to help not just my friends and my family. Since the beginning of the year I started training unemployed people to be able to go back to work. It is one of the most rewarding things I have done in my life (only beaten by having children on my own through IVF – but that's a different story).

Everyone can find a course or a trainer, a mentor or a coach. See if they have achieved what you want to achieve and work with them to set your targets and your steps. Hopefully, they can hold you accountable every step of the way and help you remain focused and disciplined, which will, therefore, achieve your desired outcome and successes.

No matter what it is that you want, there is a solution! It might require you to think outside the box, but once you do, then the possibilities are endless. How do you get the type of mindset that will have you focused on solutions?

It starts by retraining your brain to look for the positive. See challenges and address them, instead of seeing obstacles that are blocking your path to success. Accept that it can be difficult to shift your mindset after years of experiences that shaped your way of looking at your world. Give yourself some credit for starting small and being persistent! (And if you have children start them as early as possible on their "yes I can do this" way through life!)

Now, you might not realize this but language also plays a huge part in your daily achievements and your thought processes. You might not immediately think about how words and language can have a massive influence, so I would like to set a challenge for you:

For seven days, stop for a few seconds every time you THINK or SAY something negative!

If you want to keep track, open a document on your mobile phone and write down how many times a day you say something negative about work, friends, your colleagues or about your health, partner, family members or whatever you think or talk about. You'll be amazed, if you are honest with yourself, by just how many times every day you think negatively and don't even realize it. Both mentally and verbally we need to make ourselves aware every hour of the day how we think and what consequences this has on our behavior, perception and actions.

Here's a challenge for the second week: stop yourself before you say something negative and consider putting it into a positive phrase.

Instead of shouting for the tenth time at your child for not having done something you asked, take a deep breath and explain the issue. Rather than scolding or punishment, which so far has never really given you the result you have wanted, find a solution to move forward.

Instead of slagging off your colleague, just say nothing or try and actually compliment him or her. Find that one positive thing that you see in him or her.

If you know that your partner "always" forgets something, is always late, or whatever he or she might do, anticipate it. Offer your help if you are better at it and find a solution together so you can both relax.

Changing both your thought processes and your language is key to any change.

Of course, some things are harder to get done on your own. That's why working with someone who can shake up your routines, who can remind you of your goals and achievements and who can re-focus you, can be a huge source of motivation. I love my job. I love helping people who are feeling stuck in a difficult situation in their lives, shifting their mindset and helping them to set and achieve their goals. Find that person that can be your 'go to Person' to move forward.

# REALIZE THE IMPACT OF YOUR HABITS, PRIORITIES AND BELIEFS

One of the realities of creating any change in your life involves recognizing how your routines, and also your habits, impact your life. That can often be harder than you realize, but once you start the process of being honest with yourself and shifting your thinking, then the impact of your habits, your priorities and your beliefs will become apparent.

One of my clients who is unemployed talked about his goal of writing his own book and opening his own small business. Throughout the process, he has taken in so much and has already moved miles forward. I am thrilled with his progress, but when we started talking about making healthy food choices, the excuses started to fly.

"I'm not good at that, it costs so much" or "What is healthy anyway?"

Every response was an excuse about why changing his eating habits was not possible. So, to help him shift his thinking, I started with something that I knew he could do, regardless of budget or time.

"Well, you can start with drinking eight free glasses of tap water every day," I said.

"Eight?"

He looked at me for a minute as if I had asked him to do something extraordinary. I confirmed that I had said eight. "Ah, I can't do this," he said.

"Why? It is free and it is so simple."

Then I shifted the topic to his dog. His eyes lit up and he spoke with such love and gratitude for his dog. "He is the one keeping me sane through my dark times, but he is old now and has hip problems," he said.

"Do you walk him every day?" I asked.

"Of course!"

"Do you feed him every day?"

"Of course!"

"And when he is thirsty, do you give him water?"

"Of course!"

"So, you look after your dog, but not yourself?"

After a long silence, he said, "Oh, I see."

Sometimes, we know what we need to do, but we don't really realize it. Or rather, we know what to do, but we choose not to act. Take the issues in your life and imagine that someone else told you about those same problems in their life. What would you say to them? What solutions would you present to them?

Write down the options that you would suggest to someone else. Then write down all your thoughts regarding the situation. Include a list of all the objections that you might have. For each objection, I challenge you to come up with one positive answer. You need to be actively searching for solutions. It is about training yourself to think in a new way, one that allows you to tap into your creative mind and the solutions that are locked up inside your mind.

The reality is that you most likely have the answers, but you are blocking them with whatever excuse you have been telling yourself. I want you to change your habits to break through those blockades. But right now, that might feel a bit overwhelming.

So, by taking small steps, you can take action daily to implement just one of the positive solutions you found. Work on them until that solution becomes one of your new habits. You will know it has truly become a habit when you don't think about it anymore, just like when you are driving a car. Then move on to the next point.

Changing a habit starts with:

- defining your goal

- finding out what your false beliefs are that hinder you and hold you back

- breaking your goal down into smaller steps

- creating a timeframe for achieving each of those smaller steps

- finding motivation by defining the "WHY"

- moving forward by completing the smaller steps

It is possible to stop habits from one day to the other, like it is possible to stop smoking, but it needs a lot more discipline and effort than many of us are willing to invest. So set for yourself small steps and small goals!

You need to actively replace every small step you set for yourself and stay focused on the solutions you have set out and defined for yourself. Each habit you replace will allow you to then shift to another one. Creating any change in your life, small or major, begins with these small changes.

Always seek positive reinforcement as that is the key to inspiring continued action. If you are trying to change everything at once, the process becomes overwhelming, and our tendency is to just give up. I want you to manage the process of change. I want the process and the small successes to motivate you and keep you moving forward.

# BE CREATIVE – LOOK FOR OPPORTUNITIES EVEN WHERE YOU WOULDN'T EXPECT THEM

This tool is priceless, from working with your children or your family to working in your job, with your team, or on your relationship.

Last week, I had to take my car to a car wash. I had to do it with my 2-year-old twins, which most parents will agree is not as easy as when you do it on your own. I had to keep my children occupied for 30 minutes so we went for a walk. Now, not many 2-year-olds are hugely keen on going for a walk. They don't see that exercise is good for everyone.

As we walked through the streets, I found an empty beer can and for the next 30 minutes, we kicked the beer can through the streets back towards the garage where the shiny clean car was waiting for us. Time had flown by, even for me, and neither the picture of an empty beer can in the street nor the vision of a walk for 30 minutes while waiting for the car to be cleaned would have thrilled anyone. This walk was different! An empty beer can made it fun.

I know, you can't kick a beer can around the office, you can't kick it around at home – but you CAN take nearly any task and break it down in chunky sizes and there will always be some kind of positive angle to it. Even if it only means you got it done and can cross it off your to do list! Feel the feeling of achievement!

## Think: What will make my work easier or even fun?

Are there areas in your life where you might be missing out because you are stuck seeing your world from a perspective that no longer serves you? I want you to stop looking at a situation from the same point of view and find other ways of tackling and thinking about this issue or situation. If you have discussed it with other people, and you are not getting any further, be creative! Imagine you were a famous person. How would he or she go about it? Or if you are less into this kind of creative thinking and more logical, then be creative on paper. Write a SWOT analysis (strengths, weaknesses, opportunities, threats) or just put a pros and cons list together.

START TODAY and your reality will start to shift! You will truly amaze yourself at the possibilities and opportunities that will come your way!

Even if your circumstances do not change right away, changing how you view those circumstances will allow for a change in attitude, which will lead to change in your life.

Every point in this chapter has focused on you finding solutions by opening your mind and shifting your perception. Now I want to question whether you are actually being honest with yourself and taking responsibility for your life choices or if you are essentially hiding with your head in the sand.

## TAKING RESPONSIBILITY STARTS WITH HONESTY

How good are you at taking responsibility for your own actions? Be honest with yourself!

Today's culture focuses on blaming others and using circumstances outside of our control as the reason why we react or behave a certain way. It's easier to feel like a victim than to take responsibility for our own actions.

Not long after I had joined a new company, which required me to move from Germany to London, my former boss told me that it was my fault that one of the hotel contractors had missed the assigned deadline. That contractor had received the deadline from me two months earlier. Her inactions meant we lost a huge piece of business. I was livid! I had gone out and gained the client's trust, asking my boss that the company spend money on a sales trip. I had done my sales job, and now I got the blame for losing the business?! The contractor hadn't even looked at the file for the whole past two months. I was at fault? Not her?

It was a learning experience for me, one that I took with me, eventually to open my own first business. First, though, I immediately changed my way of working. Every request was put into a separate file. I started keeping count of the work that I had passed to the contributing departments. I started to chase everything! I was determined that this was never going to happen to me again.

## Think: Always take responsibility!

Today as a business owner, I can better understand my former boss's point of view. It was a big piece of business, one that needed to be managed and monitored throughout the process and that should have been my job and, of course, it was in my interest to check for updates. However, I also learnt that if a member of staff can be allowed to sit on a piece of business with no one checking on the progress, then process and management also need to be checked and changed. The internal systems of each business, of course, also need to be thoroughly reviewed and analyzed.

Today, therefore, the first person I always hold accountable is myself. The responsibility for the success or failure of my businesses always lies first and foremost with me. When you are trying to make a significant change in your life or career, it can be difficult to be honest with yourself and acknowledge how you may have contributed to an outcome you didn't desire. Without that acknowledgment and honesty, however, you cannot learn and grow from your experiences.

You might not always like what you find, but if you are not honest with yourself, then you can't make changes, create a different outcome or move forward.

## Think: What can I do to move things forward and what is my responsibility?

If you truly want change in your life, analyze each section and ask yourself honestly what your current status quo is.

What are you willing to accept from yourself? Where do you want to go and WHO do you want to be or become? Whether it be in family life, as a parent, as a boss, as a colleague, in your sports achievement or as a partner. Create your vision!

Push yourself out of your comfort zone! Yes, it might sometimes be uncomfortable!

It definitely was uncomfortable to hear what my boss had to say, but it allowed me to rethink my way of working, my way of thinking and to do what was necessary to change and improve the situation, both then and in my future. Mistakes are there to be made but make them just once!

Here are a few questions to help you start shifting your thinking into solution-based thinking and help you identify the ways that you might be falling into the "blame game":

- What do or did I contribute to my current circumstances, both personally and professionally?

- Have I been open to taking risks and stepping outside of my comfort zone?

- Where am I blaming others, or circumstances, rather than taking responsibility to move forward?

- Are the things that are holding me back in the past and therefore cannot be changed?

- How can I accept the past and learn to move forward?

- What small step can I set today to move me on the road for change and success?

Are you willing to break out of your comfort zone? Are you willing to really be honest with yourself? Only you are in charge of your life and it is important to take responsibility for it!

## WHAT IS THE BLAME GAME?

I want to stop for a minute and talk about the blame game. Simply put, it is when you are dealing with various situations in your life and choose to blame others for your situation. You believe you are the victim, instead of focusing on what you could do to change the situation NOW. You are essentially giving away your power and allowing others to control your life. The thought process turns into one that makes everything appear impossible and out of your control, so you sit, stuck, doing nothing at all to create change in your life.

I see some of this in my clients that are unemployed. The system especially twenty or more years ago wasn't set up to identify ADHD or dyslexia or other forms of learning disabilities. Parents might have not been able to help financially or mentally and once someone is at the bottom it really is hard to get up again. Not to mention, many companies do not even give people a chance to prove themselves.

However, this absolutely does not mean you should give up! The past is the past and can never be changed. Now is the time to take responsibility, move forward, make changes, listen, learn, forgive and make that leap! Be responsible, be on time, be reliable and be flexible! All these actions anyone can do, regardless of your situation.

Here are some questions to ask yourself as you deal with various situations in your life:

- Do you blame someone for something in your life?

- Do you blame a situation for something that went wrong in your life?

- Do you appear to take responsibility, but then turn around and immediately start focusing on the actions of others?

- Do you compare your choices and actions with others, judging them as better or worse?

- Are you letting others rule your life?

- Are you not taking action because you believe nothing can be done?

**Think: Let the past lie, accept what cannot be changed and take action to have that better future you deserve!**


## CREATING ACTIONS

No matter what circumstances we all are presented with in life, we still have the ability to act. You still control your thoughts and feelings. No one else has that control, nor should they! Even in old age you can take action, so age is no excuse! Do not become so focused on finding excuses that you block yourself from opening doors and creating opportunities for yourself.

A few weeks ago, as I sat to have a relaxing manicure, the TV screen on the wall showed a Ninja UK program where amazing young men and women go over very intense courses, challenging their own fitness, agility and power. One candidate even had only one leg.

A very big lady sitting next to me said, "Oh, I want him to win. How amazing is he!"

When coming across one exercise, which was already hugely difficult for the candidates with two legs, he failed and fell into the pool below.

The lady turned around to her waiting husband and said, "Wow, that makes me want to go to the gym."

Not in a million years did I think that she would go home and start working out. You WISH you were as fit, but you are unwilling to put in the hard work. Instead, we spend our energy coming up with excuses for why things can't get done. The reality is that you are making up reasons why you won't do it.

## Think: What excuses are you using to justify why you aren't taking action?

There are so many excuses that we create to justify why we refuse to act and create change in our lives. Why do we wish for things but then take no action?

- Because it seems too hard.

- Because it seems too tiring.

- Because there does not seem to be enough time.

- Because, because, because.....

The list is long. However, there is so much that is possible when you only open up your mind and heart!

**Think: The possibilities in my life are endless if I only embrace them!**

Inaction, a lack of honesty with yourself and not taking responsibility are just a few of the key reasons why you might be struggling to create change in your life. By acknowledging how these reasons contribute to your current situation, you begin to change. Once you decide to change your thinking and perception, then you need to find others who support you in these efforts.

## NETWORKING: BUILDING SUPPORT FOR CHANGE

One of the things so many people are afraid of seems to be networking. What is it about going to an event and talking to strangers that people worry about? Everyone is there for the same reasons. What is the worst that can happen?

You can expand your network and increase the resources available to you professionally and personally. New networks are also great ways to find individuals who can help hold you accountable or even offer you different choices for work or life. Also remember, these people also know others who might be able to help with your challenges and efforts or, of course, you can help them!

I constantly encourage people to look at who they are surrounding themselves with. Be honest with yourself about the type of thinking they represent.

**Think: Is it the type of thinking you want to make a part of your life? Do THEY lead the life you want for yourself?**

Leave "friends" behind that shoot people down. They are no friends if they don't support you. They only keep you around to make themselves feel better by belittling you. Move on, there are new people to be met who will believe in what you want to achieve, and who live and breathe the solutions you need.

The people you surround yourself with can also serve as inspiration. They can get you motivated to keep tackling various challenges in your life, instead of giving up. Feelings of frustration can become blockades in your efforts to be solution oriented in your thinking.

Our inner circle, those people who support us, can be the way that you break through frustration, barriers and problems. They might even provide a few solutions you never thought of.

The more you surround yourself with solution-focused individuals, the more you will think in solutions. The same is true when you are trying to change habits or create new ones. Let's talk about how to shift them without being overwhelmed in the process.

Building a network involves finding places with like-minded individuals, be it personally or professionally. If you are looking to build a professional network, then start with industry events where you can meet other professionals who can point you to various opportunities.

Personal networking often starts with self-empowerment and growth opportunities. It could be mastermind classes or attending talks specifically focused on areas that you are trying to grow in. The point of any class or talk is about not only learning, but meeting others. You make connections that help you grow, but you might also prove to be a connection that allows them to grow.

Why should you build a network?

Here are a few of the key reasons:

- to help you explore new solutions to your challenges

- to help you meet others with different perspectives

- to challenge yourself to stretch your abilities

- for support in making shifts, personally or professionally

- to find the people to help you grow and become successful in what you want to do

- to give advice and support to others who may be in a situation similar to one you are or were in

Networking opportunities are available in a variety of areas. You can opt to search online for networking opportunities, such as those for local business owners. If you are looking for opportunities to create change in the community, then look for community get-togethers where you can meet others and build support. Or find a local charity, a new sport you can take up – the opportunities are endless.

The point is that finding networking opportunities often starts by just opening your mind and having the willingness to extend yourself beyond your current status quo. I always encourage people to build or extend their network, because doing so will give more opportunities to grow and learn. You might be thinking, "I don't have time to network. My schedule is already so full."

I understand what it means to be a busy professional. Being a single mother to my truly amazing twins and running my businesses, as well as all of my other professional endeavors, means that my schedule often seems to be running me. To make time for new networking opportunities every now and then, I have focused on prioritizing, systemizing, working hard and, where possible, delegating. It helps me to manage all my obligations and to make time for everything in my life that I find valuable, both personally and professionally. And if you still find it daunting to go networking, then come on our networking course or search for one in your area.

# FINDING MOTIVATION IN YOUR LIFE

We all need motivation. I think of it as the key necessary to get the car started. Without it, you are not going anywhere. You don't start you go nowhere! However, once you start every small success will feed more success and in return will fuel your motivation.

The idea is to keep yourself motivated through the progress you make. Another way to remain motivated is of course through mentors or coaches.

Once I stared looking for and working with my mentors I truly got inspired and motivated to tackle the challenges in my life and find my solutions. Mentors keep you on your toes, and for me they continue to show me new ways of thinking that inspire me to learn and grow; every day!

Not only is it important to work with mentors, you also learn when you teach yourself. Mentoring others gives you a chance to reinforce, in your own mind, the ways that you want to think and act.

Taking action involves work, but once you get started, you will be amazed at how much better you feel. Your world will start to change because you have changed your way of thinking.

Do not be afraid to take the first steps to create change by shifting your thinking and perceptions. Once you make that shift, then you are going to find it easier to build a network, change your habits and start on the path of growth and finding solutions. My professional life benefited when I stopped making excuses or finding others to blame. The lessons I learned carried into my businesses and my personal life have assisted me in every goal that I have achieved so far.

No matter where you are in terms of your personal or professional life, do not assume that it is too late to take risks or that you cannot change. You have the power of YES to create the life that you want. It starts by changing your thinking, from searching for problems to being solution oriented.

**Connect with Astrid and her team at www.solutions-finder.com and share your journey with them to find the solutions for your challenges. On the website you can share stories, learn about Astrid's events, and become the more successful YOU!**

# From Pain to Powerful

## GLENN EDWARDS

*"You have the power to heal your life, and you need to know that. We think so often that we are helpless, but we're not. We always have the power of our minds… Claim and consciously use your power."*

– Louise L. Hay

## YOU ARE YOUR POWER

When all goes wrong, how do you use your power to heal?

When you feel like you have no fight left, how do you call on your power to lift you up?

When you think you can't take any more, how do you remind yourself that you do have power?

I have learned a lot in this lifetime, as we all do when we're open to the lesson. But I believe the most important one is that I always have the power to heal. It is a choice and it's my choice. The same goes for you too. YOU HAVE A CHOICE. You can either let anger, regret, loss, disappointment, and fear steal your power away, or you can use your power to heal.

It's on you! Make the choice to live in your misery or do the work. It took me a while to learn this lesson. Now that I have, I can't unlearn it. I have actively made the choice to not only live in positivity, but to be a positive light for others as well. Don't get me wrong here, the fact that I choose to be positive doesn't mean that I don't recognize or deal with my negative emotions. They are there. I feel them. Some of them are the effect of a cause that's based in reality and some of them are born out of anxiety. They exist. I do the work to turn them around.

Positivity isn't magic. It's not a mythical creature in a story with a fairy-tale ending. You can create your own happily(ish)-ever-after. I know it because I've done it and my life is no stranger to tragedy.  Oh and I say happily(ish) because, let's be real here, the whole idea of happily-ever-after is misleading. It leads the audience to assume that everything from that point on was perfection, but life will never be perfect. There will always be challenges. There will always be work to do. Living with a positive outlook isn't about arriving at a destination, it's a continuous exploration. It's one that I am excited to embark on every single day.

# LOSING MYSELF

Like I said, I am no stranger to tragedy and loss. My family has lived through the double homicide of my aunt and uncle, drug addiction, rape, divorce (she just walked away after 33 years), and the alienation of my 5 grandchildren.

As these things were happening to me and all around me, I suppressed my emotions. I was that guy: the confident one who could walk into a room and make others laugh. I had grown two successful businesses and was an inspiration to others who wanted to do the same. I loved to goof off and joke around. All the while I was dying on the inside. I hated the word negative and actually still do, but my relationship with the word has changed. Before I began to work on myself, I suppressed my negative emotions, allowing them to fester and grow. Now I deal with them, and use my power to heal. It is in the healing that I have become a more positive, joyful, and abundant person.

What changed? What made me realize I needed help? What was my turning point?

It was that moment when I realized I had lost myself so completely and entirely that I had created an exit plan. I was ready to die. I was ready to commit suicide. I had hit a point where everything felt like too much. I was overwhelmed by anger and sadness. The hurt that I had been suppressing for years had bubbled to the surface, causing an uncontrollable rage within me that was coming out in ways that made me feel like someone else entirely. I had lost myself in it.

Even in those moments when I was ready to kill myself, I realized it wasn't right. I never, ever thought that I would want that. I knew I had so much to be grateful for in my life and yet I couldn't see past the horrible things that had happened not only to myself, but the people I loved.

Until one day, a realization broke through the noise. It was a whisper at first and I almost didn't even hear it. It said, "You don't actually want to die. You have so much life left. Are you really ready to miss out on all this world has left to offer you?"

I am now so incredibly grateful that I heard the whisper. If I hadn't, I wouldn't be here today to understand just how much I would've left behind. That one powerful thought made me realize that I was the only one who could turn things around. I had to make the choice to pick myself up, seek the help I needed and do the work to heal.

I've done the work and continue to do the work.

MY life is worth it and so am I.

YOUR life is worth it and so are you.

## OWN YOUR POWER

Owning the power within yourself begins with accepting all that you are. This acceptance will allow you to recognize the aspects of you that you love and want to strengthen, while helping you also to understand the aspects of your personality that you don't love and want to work on. No one is perfect. No one makes all the right decisions. Accept your flaws and know that, no matter what, you are a work in progress, one that is worth the effort.

One of the results of not working on my emotional responses to the external circumstances I faced daily was rage. Years of repression caught up with me and manifested in a lack of emotional control. I couldn't contain my anger. There was too much that had built up over time. It began exploding out of me. I didn't like it. It didn't feel good. It made me feel less than the person I had always thought I was. It diminished my power.

Once I made the choice to live, I knew that my life depended on me dealing with my pain. The time to face it had come. I knew I needed help, and as I learned throughout the process, it was important to seek the right kind of help. The first step for me was to deal with my rage.

I had been to visit my daughter, who had been battling drug addiction and was in rehab, when it hit me. If she had the strength she needed to beat drugs, then I too could beat my rage and live a more positive life.

I began my search for help by going to my doctor and explaining what my emotional outbursts felt like. He immediately referred me to meet with a social worker. It was completely unacceptable. The social worker couldn't even begin to comprehend the level of help I required. My case was over his head, and so I had to go back to my doctor and advocate for my needs.

He then sent me to a psychiatrist who worked with rage. If you don't know exactly what rage is, that's okay. You really don't want to. There are two types of rage: explosion and implosion. I was experiencing the explosive version and it was not pretty. If the line was crossed, really, really bad things, such as years or possibly a lifetime of jail, could happen. I worked so hard not to cross that line.

The first psychiatrist I met with purposely tried to instigate a rage, so that he could capture it on camera. What?!? I was floored. Did he not understand? He was the only one in the room with me. Did he really think he could control me? I didn't want to find out. I wanted help, and his methods were only serving to make things worse. Even the second psychiatrist, his partner, couldn't understand why he would do this.

It took me a few more tries to find the psychiatrist that worked for me and who ultimately gave me the tools I needed to continue to work on myself. My point in telling you this story is that you really need to make sure the help you need is the help you're getting. Although it may feel like an overwhelming challenge when you're not feeling well, you have to be a strong advocate for yourself.

One of the most worrisome aspects of the healthcare system, the way it is set up today, is that there seems to be little to no accountability, especially within the area of mental health. What this means is that often psychiatrists do not have the skills to treat all of the patients they are presented with. In my case, I found that they would hear me, but not necessarily listen to me, and then at the end of it all they would say there was nothing they could do for me. What a colossal waste of time! Not only that, but it was incredibly disheartening.

What I've learned to do is ask the psychiatrist flat out if they can handle my case. I let them know how important it is that they not take me on if they can't help. I let them know it's okay if they can't help and ask them to research and recommend a specialist who can.

People need to slow down and listen. If you feel you're not being heard then you need to find someone who will listen to you, and I mean authentically listen to your individual story and personalized needs. ADVOCATE FOR YOURSELF!

Understanding and working through my emotions in order to control my rage was only a small part of the work I did to turn my life around. I also sought the expertise of life coaches, like Raymond Aaron, who have helped me realize that, while I do have a fulfilling life, I am still playing small. I could be doing more.

While I write this chapter I am fast approaching my 60th birthday. Not everyone thinks that, at this age, it's time to achieve new goals. I do. Changing my perspective from being one that was stuck in negativity to one that is now filled with positivity has opened up a whole new world of possibility. I am ready to embark on this new adventure and share my journey with you, all because I decided that I wasn't ready to give up on my life. In doing this, I began to truly own my power in a way that I have never done so before.

Some of the lessons I learned on my own healing journey that I would like to share with the world are:

1. Know your core values.

2. Communication is key.

3. Accept yourself and treat yourself with compassion.

4. Forgive yourself for letting things go.

5. You have to heal in order to recover.

6. There is always a positive.

7. Be transparent.

8. The best place to live is in your dash.

9. It is never too late to live your best life.

## KNOW YOUR CORE VALUES

Do you know your core values? You know, the ones you live by. The ones that help you make the tough decisions. The ones that keep you on that life path that is uniquely yours.

I have found that most people don't. When I ask people I get a range of responses from I don't think about that stuff to oh, I dunno… to yeah, I guess it would be something like love and honesty.

A lot of people really don't sit down to think about their core values. I mean really think about them, define them, and understand how living by them can truly change their life. Your core values are a bit like those signs that let you know where to turn when you're headed towards the airport. Heading to the airport? Yes, turn right in 500 meters. Perfect! Now you know exactly where you're going.

Why wouldn't you want to know what your core values are? They are essentially your internal road map, especially during the really bad times when it's easy to veer off course. I've done the work to define my core values and it has helped immensely in not only healing my past pain, but in helping me deal with hurt as it happens in the moment.

How do you know what your core values are? Take some time and think about what means most to you in your life. Is it love? Is it health? Is it creativity? Is it discovery? Your core values are unique to you, and no book can tell you exactly what they are. That is something you have to decide for yourself.

The top 6 core values that guide me are:

- Honesty

- Compassion

- Integrity

- Clarity

- Calm

- Fun

Once you have a general idea, you need to go deeper. For example, what exactly do I mean by honesty? Sure, it seems simple: always tell the truth. I'm almost 100% sure everyone reading this learned how to tell a lie very early in life, especially when busted doing something their parents had specifically told them not to. Go deeper than that! For me, honesty means not only being honest with others, but being honest with myself.

It is so easy to lie to myself. I am brilliant at it! Or, I used to be anyway. Now, I look a little more closely. A simple example: I lost $300 dollars at the casino in 20 minutes a few months back. Ouch! I quickly reached for my wallet, telling myself I could easily make it back.

What a liar! Obviously, I couldn't easily make it back or I wouldn't have lost it in the first place. The truth is that gambling, being a game of chance, offered me the opportunity to win it back, but only if I was willing to lose more money. I wasn't. I put my wallet back where it belonged!

Go through each core value and flesh it out. These are your guides. They will keep you on a life path that brings you more joy and less pain, as long as you let them.

## COMMUNICATION IS KEY

Bottling up your feelings and expecting others to understand why you're hurt is one of the best ways to ensure that you will never heal. Communicate your emotions. Talk about your feelings. If you're upset with someone, tell them. Just because you feel something doesn't make it right. You may be completely misinterpreting the other person's words or actions. Ask them why they did it. Ask them what they're feeling. Talk it out.

Three components to open communication:

1.   Honest and authentic sharing.

2.   Active listening.

3.   Coming together.

All can be a challenge. Most people don't share what they have to say because they think no one cares. I disagree. I think the right people care, even if what you're telling them is hard to hear.

You have to be willing to listen to what they have to say too. Communication is never one-sided. If you're speaking and not hearing, you're just talking at someone and you'll never achieve authentic communication. You have to listen actively. That means tuning in with your thoughts while the other person is speaking and making sure you haven't let them wander away from listening. One of the biggest mistakes people make is listening with the intent to respond. This isn't real listening. Listen, just to listen. If you need time to think about your response, that's okay, take what you need. It isn't a movie. There isn't an audience waiting for a snappy reply.

I wish that my daughter would talk to me about why I had to lay off her husband. She's never even tried to talk to me about it. She doesn't want to know why because she doesn't care. This is an example of what happens when communication breaks down. As you can see, even though I've done the work to heal and live with a more positive outlook, life isn't perfect. I still can't reach my daughter, and I miss my grandkids every day.

My daughter's inability to communicate her feelings to me has caused her to use her children as a weapon, which I personally feel is child abuse. It's fine for her to be mad at me. Adults fight. But adults also resolve their issues through sharing their feelings and listening to the other person's side. It hurts. But in order to heal, you have to deal with the hurt. What adults should never do is bring innocent children into the mix of their adult fight. It isn't right. I wish she would just talk to me instead.

## ACCEPT YOURSELF AND TREAT YOURSELF WITH COMPASSION

One of hardest things for me to do as I worked on healing was to accept that I was at one time willing to take my own life. I had always seen myself as strong, successful, confident, and filled with an unwavering passion for life. My desire to end it all shook me to my core. How could someone who was proud of living a full life want to give it all up without a fight?

Once I was able to accept that part of myself, I was able to move forward in my own healing. Not only that, but I had to accept my anger, understand why I was angry, and show myself some compassion. It is acceptance combined with compassion that will see you through to the healing you not only need but deserve.

Yes, you deserve to heal. Some of the reasons you might be stopping yourself from healing are:

- You don't want to deal with the pain.

- You are suppressing your emotions in order to not hurt others.

- You are afraid of looking too closely at the cause of your hurt.

- You are uncertain of what a future without the pain will look like.

- You are comfortable living in your misery.

Does any of this sound like you? I know that at one point or another in my life, all of it sounded like me. I lived in my pain and suffering for so long. I got by and still managed on the outside to project a life of success and happiness. That outward projection, as you've seen, couldn't have been more wrong.

Take a moment and understand why you've chosen not to allow yourself to heal from past pain. Think about how it is affecting your life, and about the joy it has stopped you from experiencing. Accept your reasons, show yourself some compassion, and make a promise to yourself to begin the healing process now.

# FORGIVE YOURSELF FOR LETTING THINGS GO

Sometimes in order to heal you need to simply let things go without a resolution. The person you feel you need an apology from in order to obtain closure is either unable or unwilling to give it. This may not feel okay, but you have to let it be; otherwise, you are the one who will live the rest of your life feeling that pain.

The man who murdered my aunt and uncle never once apologized. I wanted an apology. Not so that I could forgive him; I don't need to forgive him. I felt like I needed it so that I could move on, especially so that I could let go of the anger that I had been carrying for so long. Long after my cousin went on to live a life her parents would be so proud of. It wasn't until I forgave myself for failing to obtain an apology from her parents' murderer that I was able to begin the healing process. It was in forgiving myself that I was able to live a more positive life.

I know this might not be what you'd expect to hear. Most people might say that they forgave the person who they needed the apology from, but for me, it was myself that I needed to forgive. So forgive yourself for letting yourself down and then let go of your need for the apology that you will never receive.

## YOU HAVE TO HEAL IN ORDER TO RECOVER

You can't go over it. You can't get around it. You can't go under it. You can't run through it blindly with your eyes closed, hoping you'll come out the other end without a few scars. You have to walk through your healing process at a pace that allows you to feel all the things you need to feel in order to heal.

Living in the pain of a new wound without the help of a painkiller, or reopening old wounds hurts. But in order to truly heal from emotional trauma, it has to be done. Whether it is death, the end of a marriage, a traumatic event, a friend who wronged you, an employer who took advantage of you, a seemingly perfect opportunity that passed you by, you have to find a way to heal.

What healing looks like for you won't be the same as what it looks like for anyone else. Compassion, acceptance and forgiveness are all great places to begin, but where do you need to go from there in your healing process? For me it was to deal with my pent up anger. With each new tragedy or loss, I let my rage take over. I had allowed it a lifetime of expansion, and so for me that was the next step in my healing process.

How has your pain held you back? Pain can manifest in feelings of guilt, low self-esteem, anger, self-pity, fear, anxiety, self-hatred… you name the horrible feeling, and your pain has a hand in it. All of these can escalate to depression, suicidal ideation, and even suicide if left to grow within you. Guilt, low self-esteem, and self-hatred can stop you from recognizing new opportunities or even taking action on the opportunities that are right there for your taking because you don't value yourself or your life. All of these feelings make you feel insignificant, and ensure that you will continue living your life small.

Heal your pain; your life depends on it! Your big, expansive, and joy-filled life is waiting.

# THERE IS ALWAYS A POSITIVE

Even in the absolute worst of situations there is a positive to be found. Yes, in death, divorce, drug addiction, and traumatic events there is always a positive.

How angry did you feel reading that? Are you ready to throw the book down and call it a day? Are you cursing my name?

Look, I am not saying that you have to turn these events into a positive. I am not one of those faux positive people who glosses over the bad in an attempt to be a positive person. In fact, I am quite the opposite. Faux positivity only serves to bury your emotions. What I am talking about is the part of the healing process when you've recognized that you need to heal, you're ready to embark on the journey, you know how to show yourself the compassion you need, and you've begun to forgive yourself for anything you need to; and so you are ready to open your eyes to all that is there.

Let me share what I mean. A few years back I had to let my son-in-law go from one of my companies. I had received multiple complaints from other staff about his uncontrollable behaviour. I even spoke with him about the issues on more than one occasion. Yet, still he continued. Maybe he thought that his connection to me kept him safe. Unfortunately, he was hurting my business. I couldn't let him continue on with the company.

Do you know how hard it is to let a family member go? The decision didn't come lightly or swiftly. I gave him every opportunity to change, and yet when I finally did have to make the hard call he looked at me and said, "Remember every action has a reaction."

Since that day I haven't been allowed to see my grandchildren.

Am I happy about the situation?

Of course not.

Do I miss them every, single day?

Of course I do.

Would I change what I did to get them back?

No, I did what was right.

Do I still feel angry about it sometimes?

YES!

But… I recognize why I'm angry. It was losing them that drove me over the edge. It was losing them that forced me to want to end my life. It was too much.

Since that time, I have taken steps to heal the pain of the loss, like participating in Facebook groups for alienated grandparents. And most importantly, I have found the positive: for six wonderful years I knew what it felt like to be a grandfather to five beautiful children. It's not an experience everyone on this earth has the pleasure to know, and I did. No one can take those years or those memories away from me. That is my positive in this situation. Having that time with my grandkids is my saving grace. I will be forever grateful for the gift of those memories.

Are you in a situation right now where it's hard to see any sort of positive? Begin to heal yourself on the inside, and the positive will become more visible.

# BE TRANSPARENT

If I'm feeling emotional or angry about something, I do my best to be transparent about where my feelings are coming from. For example, if I've had an annoying commute into work and I know I'm grumpy I'll let my staff know that my mood has nothing to do with them.

Some people believe that being an open book can take away your power. This hasn't been my experience. I believe that transparency allows you to own your power. You accept all aspects of yourself and so there's nothing to hide.

Silence hurts.

Silence causes misunderstandings.

Silence makes us think things are worse than they are.

Silence causes arguments to escalate.

Silence causes pain to grow.

Communication has the ability to heal all wounds, as long as both parties are willing to listen. When you are open, honest, and lay everything on the table you allow yourself to be fully seen. You are giving of yourself in a vulnerable yet powerful way by letting everyone in on who you are and why you respond to things the way you do.

If I come home in a bad mood because someone at work upset me but

I don't say anything, my partner could think it's her fault. She can't read my mind. Rather than letting those thoughts fester and cause even more misunderstanding, I would rather let her know why I'm feeling grumpy and let her support me. Only good can come from this.

Communication is everything. Be transparent and watch how your interactions with others improve.

# THE BEST PLACE TO LIVE IS IN YOUR DASH

*"Your life is made of two dates and a dash. Make the most of the dash."*

– Linda Ellis

This quote resonates with me like no other. There is no better place to live than in your dash. It's the place where life exists. It's the place where you get to make your mark in the world. It's the place where you get to experience all the great things this life has to offer you.

If I had chosen to take matters into my own hands and make my second date earlier than it should've been, I would've missed out on so much. With open eyes, I met a woman who inspires me, brings me so much joy, gives her love freely, and accepts me for who I am.

I am so incredibly grateful that I am here to experience this leg of the journey. There is so much richness in my life. I am also so grateful to myself for not giving up on me. I've forgiven myself for wanting to end everything and have done so much work to live in the positive.

Take it from someone who has been on the other side of trauma: no matter what you've been through, you too can live a positive and fulfilling life. You have to do the work! If you want to live your best life, it's time to take on your pain and heal.

Recognize your pain.

Admit you need to change.

Accept yourself.

Forgive yourself.

Communicate.

Find the positive.

Live your best life every single day!

# IT'S NEVER TOO LATE TO LIVE YOUR BEST LIFE

*"There are powers inside of you which, if you could discover and use, would make of you everything you ever dreamed or imagined you could become."*

–Orison Swett Marden

You are your power! Sometimes you need some inspiration to help you head down a positive path. You can make a choice to wallow in your pain, or you can do the work. It's easy to choose not to do the work, but living through each day will be hard.

It's never too late to make the choice to live your best life. I've had many passions in my life, from playing pro hockey to being in the best shape of my life at 60, to running two successful businesses to being a husband, I am no stranger to taking on new and exciting endeavours. My most recent passions are public speaking and writing. I have a story to share and it's one that inspires others to live their best life.

When I was suffering in the dark and looking for help I found that there wasn't enough out there. It was a lonely place to be. I want to be the light in the dark for those like me who can't find the help they need. More of us need to share our story so that others can heal. It is through publishing and speaking that I do that. As a speaker I am engaging, transparent, honest, and informative. To find out more about booking me for your event, check out my website: glennedwards.ca

For now, I will leave you with a few questions to get you thinking about where you are at in your healing process:

1. Is there a hurt you have been holding onto that is stopping you from living your best life?

2. Do you forgive yourself for letting go of your hurt? Do you need to work on your communication skills?

3. Are you willing to do the work?

4. Are you ready to let go and live an amazing life.

Do the work!

I can help. Reach out and let's chat.

**To learn more about Glenn or to connect with him about speaking at your next event, visit glennedwards.ca**

# Gone, But Not Without Hope

## MONICA MONTGOMERY

*Never give up and be confident in what you do. There may be tough times,*
*but the difficulties which you face will make you more determined to achieve your*
*objectives and to win against all the odds.*

– Marta

Although I am sharing my journey with you in the following pages that reflect challenges which you could consider as negative influences, keep in mind that life is 10% of what happens to you and 90% of how you react to it. While I cannot change my past, I look to the future tomorrows and claim them as mine to win. Are you ready to stop letting your past determine where you're going?

I have found that though my life has not been long in years to this point, if I do not take the time to examine each day in my life seeing what is good and focusing on how to create a lifestyle strong in every aspect, the negative mindsets may creep in.

# IN THE BEGINNING – MY STORY

It was in the early summer, of 1996, Oaxaca, Mexico, and although I was only three months old, my life was about to change in ways no child should ever know. My brother and sister, Nick and Angel, were both with me in this desolate place, that I now had to call home.

People always tell me that I should write a book about my life and my challenges, so that I can help others who may be healing from similar stories. I honestly don't really remember most of my childhood. But, I guess, as human beings we tend to set aside the bad memories…you know, the old saying, out of thought, out of mind.

We all try to forget things that we do not want to remember, but, does anyone actually forget? I try to remember sometimes. I really do. However, maybe we need to allow our hearts and minds an escape from the realities that are and were, so painful.

My life included both a biological father, Antonio and a stepfather, Luis. My biological father, Antonio was loathsome. It was Mom's first marriage and she loved him dearly. But, the day came after watching him change so radically, and she discovered the truth. Not only was she saddened, but also repulsed with what she learned. He had been using the name and social identification number of a dead man! Who had she been married to? What name was hers to use, and who had she been living with all that time? What scum, to have mislead her like that, to lie to the woman he promised to love and cherish. It repulses me to even think about him. On top of that…who knows what his name actually was.

Antonio was more than just a contemptible person. He was evil. But, it was not evident until long after my mother had been married to him, that she discovered there was something in his character causing him to be relentless and to possess a profound wickedness in his behavior.

I suppose, as with most marriages, it started out perfectly, as a family living in an extraordinary home together, and with three healthy beautiful children. They were happy and the ideal family that everyone envied.

After a few years together, he began getting into the drug game…and I do not mean in a small way. But larger than before with even greater risks, putting his family in jeopardy from the thugs, cartel, and mafia that he associated with. He had no concern for our safety, or he would have never kidnapped us, or put our three lives in complete peril. Not only was he selling cocaine but using it himself. Mom thinks that is what changed him into the monster he became. She describes what she had found one day, as a large bag of white powder. She had grown tired of the drug presence in her home and bothered by the change she witnessed in his personality. She even tried to get rid of the drugs by flushing them down the toilet, but he somehow found out, or perhaps he was there; I'm not quite sure. He slapped my mom across the face, showing no emotion and time did not improve life for my mother, as the abuse continued. She knew that he was no longer the man she had married.

My mother was terrified to make a move or try to take us away. He had threatened to kill her or take us away from her. He even killed my brother's cat in front of us to prove he was serious. He was a powerful and influential man, so she believed his threats. But she quietly stashed away the supplies and money she needed to escape to a safer location, departing as soon as it was safe.

We were off to Dallas, Texas, where we finally felt we would be safe again. However, little did we know we were far from safe.

## KIDNAPPED WITH NOWHERE TO GO

Having been kidnapped at such a young age with my brother and sister, this was a traumatic time in all of our lives. We were toddlers and not aware of what was happening.

My brother, Nick, and my sister Angel and I were abducted by my father, Antonio, which we learned was not his name. When we were older, we questioned why he even wanted us. I was not able to see much of my brother and sister during our imprisonment, as they were kept in a chicken coop and likely restrained, to keep them from running away but, my memory does not allow me the indulgence of remembering clearly.

My Mom had dropped us off at the daycare on her way to her second job. My father, Antonio, showed up and simply told them he was our father, shared his identification with the staff and they released us to him. I guess kidnapping was not such a big deal back then or of a real concern, so they just released us into his custody.

My father had taken us to a remote house in Mexico for almost five years and the departure to Mexico was a harrowing experience. My memory that I do have of Mexico is of an old rusty sink, where my days and nights had been spent. I honestly don't know why I had to sit in the sink. Probably so no one would have to change me, but who really knows. We had so many questions as to why we were made to do the things that happened there or why we were treated as we were. Maybe that saying is true…out of sight, out of mind. I even wondered why we were taken. In my mind, it must have only been, just another way to hurt my mom. Days and nights were long and lonely for us and my father was busy with strangers at odd hours of the night. I knew later in life it was due to him being big in the drug trafficking business, and likely why we were in Mexico for five years, keeping us all apart from our mother.

From the time I was a baby until the age of five, the only emotions I could feel were wrapped around confusion and were those of sadness from missing my mom, the fear of where we were, all the new faces around me, and not really having anyone to love me. I questioned in my own mind as to where my mother was and who the many strangers were that drifted in and out of our home.

Our mom searched desperately to find us, but every time she got close, he would find out. He would then send his men to hurt her. A group of men would approach our mom and tell her that they had me and that my father couldn't deal with my crying, so he just threw me away. They let her hear a baby crying on the phone, which made her become so frantic, driving her even more so to find us. She felt there was no choice but to believe them. Mom went with the thugs and ended up chained to a water heater in a basement for over a year. The torments she endured were unspeakable but that is not my story to tell.

One of the men who held her captive, must have felt some remorse for her despicable living conditions and having to chain her back up. I suppose it was due to her being near the brink of death, starving and being so cut up. His remorse led him to leave her chains unlocked one day. And, while in her weakened condition, she managed to climb out of the basement window where she limped down the road. Luckily, my mom came upon a nice older couple who had seen her in trouble and took her to a local hospital.

Through everything she went through, she never gave up. Mom persisted in selling her home, and all of her worldly possessions, using what money she could raise to hire a private investigator. I am unclear about how much time passed before the investigator was able to locate us, but I wish I knew his name. He had shown mom pictures of us, which made her weep because we had gotten so big and she had lost precious years from our childhood lives.

But, it was not that easy. They had to wait for the perfect moment to grab us and carefully do so without witnesses, for fear of a violent confrontation. They could not risk Antonio finding out, causing an uproar and moving us. Patiently, they waited, watching until they could make their next move. My father was at work, and his mother was supposed to be taking care of us but, she was passed out in the back room. That's when mom saw her opportunity. As soon as mom crept through the door, I knew exactly who she was. I knew she'd come back and had not forgotten us. I shouted momma! She asked where my brother and sister were being kept. I told her that they were outside in the chicken coop. She quickly grabbed all of us and we left. Free at last from bondage after five long agonizing years.

We got onto a large bus, as that's where the private investigator left us. As kids, we had grown up speaking only Spanish. Mom told us to be quiet as we departed because if the officials had heard us, she could have been charged with kidnapping her own children. Crazy, right?

We traveled to San Antonio where mom had met Luis, and where this part of our lives had all begun. Now, I'm not sure if my mom has horrible taste in men, or just awful luck. I don't really remember much of him at Twin Lakes in San Antonio, except for a few specific memories. To be honest, I don't remember how we left him or ended up at that shelter. I thought they just got into a fight or didn't like each other anymore. No one told me anything until some years later.

Luis was an evil man, and I am relieved that he was charged with one of the worst atrocities that any child should ever endure. I do not know how much time he served in prison, but he molested my sister, and he was found guilty of the charges. However, I never came forward that Luis had molested me as well, so no additional sentence was handed down allowing him to walk away free from the harm brought to my life. He served time because my sister stepped up and testified against him. I only wish now, that I had as well. But, another reason I had never told my mother was that it had gone on for some time and I did not realize that this wasn't normal behavior until years later when it was openly discussed.

Perhaps Luis would have served a longer term in prison if I had spoken up. My reason at the time was that I did not want my mother to be hurt about the fact two of her daughters were abused by the monster she had brought into our lives. I could never and would never blame her. For me, at the time, it was enough that Luis would never be a part of our family again.

I would like to tell all of you who have suffered at the hands of a twisted and deviant person to speak out. It is not your fault and you have done nothing wrong.

I researched the Internet for the proper meaning of the term molestation and here is what I found:

Child sexual abuse-from https://en.wikipedia.org/wiki/Child_sexual_abuse. Child sexual abuse, also called child molestation, is a form of child abuse in which an adult or older adolescent uses a child for sexual stimulation. Forms of child sexual abuse include engaging in sexual activities with a child (whether by asking or pressuring, or by other means).

## LIFE IN THE SHELTER

We stayed in a shelter which played a critical part in our recovery as a family by helping us find ourselves. The shelter is designed to aid abused mothers and their children. It gave us a warm, dry location to call home, a roof over our heads and neighbors that became our friends. It was our safe haven where we found a new beginning along with our independence to stand on our own. It is with many thanks to the shelter, the ability to regain our independent lives was made possible again. Their formal name is SAMMinistries. Their purpose is to prevent homelessness in San Antonio through a compassionate, holistic approach that brings self-sufficiency, pride, and dignity to struggling families with nowhere else to turn. (www.samm.org)

We were able to acquire our independence and our first apartment, which I believe was located on West Avenue, due to the assistance of this shelter.

My memories of our time at the shelter, remain in pieces but I have heard that your mind protects you from memories that were unbearable or shields us from parts of our lives we may not have the skills or the knowledge of how to cope. Although I have only fragments to share, it is important to me that I do.

My fragmented memory is still vague but the following are a few that stand out for me.....

- There was a clown family that lived right across the way from us.

Regina, her parents and her sociopathic brother who liked to kill little birds for fun, were amongst the most colorful and memorable neighbors. Unfortunately, they earned their living as clowns, and that was very unlucky for my mom as she was terrified of clowns. I mean, really terrified! She would literally panic, passing out at the very sight of the clowns. Luckily, they never came by dressed in their costumes.

- I also remember a Christmas holiday when my stepfather, Luis, and his mother Theresa, who stayed with us in our three-bedroom trailer. I specifically remember her, and I can almost picture it if I close my eyes, but not entirely. She was with us that Christmas wearing a dress with large purple unappealing flowers printed all over it. But, I'm not sure why I remember her. I don't think anything awful or impressive happened that Christmas for me. I just remember her sitting on a brown couch, watching us open our presents. Happily, I had received a Mickey Mouse bike, or maybe it was a scooter.

- Theresa lived in an apartment where we would go visit her from time to time. I remember one visit we had to walk down a long hallway just to get to her door. I liked to help when I could do grown-up things, but she was not always kind. One memory I have is standing at the sink on a chair because I was too short to reach the counter. My hands were not very big, being a small child, I accidentally dropped one of her expensive dishes, breaking it. Theresa got so angry, slapping my face really hard and sending me to remain seated on the couch until mom came to get us. She yelled at me saying, I do not want your help any longer. I cried as I waited for my mom to pick us up, which felt like forever, wishing we never had to visit her again.

I remember a couple of buildings down from our apartment, we attended church early in the mornings. A girl named Elena, and her mom held the church for the kids living in the apartments and even provided us with snacks and gifts on Christmas. One Christmas she had decided to teach all of us a lesson. She had wrapped presents and put them under the tree for when we arrived…. they were both very large and small looking gifts. She allowed each of us to go one at a time, selecting the present we had most wanted, but of course, we had no idea of what was in any of them. I picked the largest box of all. Well, c'mon I was a child and I thought it was an easy bake oven. Anyway, my huge present turned out to be an assortment of canned food but the gifts that were the smaller gifts turnout to be the best ones! They all had money or even something better. As a small girl, it was difficult to understand but, bigger is not always better!  The moral of the story was invaluable and a lesson I will always remember.

When we had left the shelter, we departed with the knowledge of many life's lessons from the staff at the shelters to new friends that we made. Another memory I would like to share is when I walked to school with a little girl named Grace, she also stayed in the complex. I believe the elementary school was also on West Avenue. But all I can remember about it is that I had dissected a starfish and then I had attended an alternative learning center with my friend, Carlos, also from the shelter.

Carlos and I had been passing notes to each other, as we were planning our revenge, on another student that had been harassing us. Our revenge was a bit over the top even though we were not really serious about what we had said and the teacher flipped out, calling the police as though we were going to murder this kid. It was all a bit excessive now that I think about it. Because the cops were called, I had to go to an alternative school for a couple of months. It was a good lesson for us that even idle threats can backfire and no matter our age, we were cautious not to react with out of control threats of behavior.

At the school, we sat in cubicles by ourselves, and had to complete packets of work pushed through a small slot in the cubby. Carlos and I also had to do community service and clean the shelter where we used to live at. We had to scrub the stairs with a toothbrush to teach us a lesson, kind of thing! I liked cleaning and I got to do it with Carlos, so it wasn't that bad. At least it was one way to think about it. However, my mom was disappointed in me, which was worse than any other punishment I could have ever received.

After living at our new apartment for a while, mom had been talking to someone named David. She spoke to him online and over the phone for some time before she had told us that he was her friend and that he lived in Houston. I remember speaking to him on the phone a few times and he sounded really nice. After a while, mom asked us what we thought about the idea of moving to Houston. It was a big step, but I think we were all ready for a change. Moving, and leaving people behind, didn't bother me much. I guess it was because I was never really that close to anyone. Plus, moving away, got me out of a huge debt from the clown girl's brother. I owed him a bunch of money. I had bought from him, the little birds he had tried to kill, and some handcuffs and other things. I told him that my mom would get her money the day we were moving and I would bring it to him. It was about three thousand dollars. But I left a note on the door saying you can have your money if you can find me. Hahahaha I thought I was so funny! Come on…you would have done the same thing! I saved birds okay…tiny, baby birds. It was justified and I thought he deserved what I had done to him.

Onward to Houston! Another move, but because I had never made any connections, I was fine with leaving. It all seemed like a great idea to me.

We moved to Houston and met David. He had both feet and both legs. You'll soon understand why I say that. When we met him, he seemed truly nice and treated mom well, so we moved in with him. But, the apartment was very tiny, which was no problem because we just slept on sofas or in the back room.

I do not really remember much about that apartment except a fight that mom and David had. He was a diabetic who did not take care of himself. Unfortunately, he accidentally stepped on a nail and punctured his foot. Since he did not take care of his wound, his foot became infected. And, being diabetic, it was very serious, causing him to lose his foot.

David and mom got into arguments frequently. This particular fight caused her to sleep in the living room. He deserved that lack of attention. I remember him crawling on his knees to go talk to her. Or, sometimes he would make her more angry so they would fight again. I'm not sure. She would storm back into the bedroom and he would crawl on his knees past the door again. He followed her back and forth a couple of times before I went to sleep.

Moving from the cramped living quarters, we took up residence at Pinemont, where we enjoyed another three-bedroom apartment. In the process of moving, I accidentally dropped a diary I owned and my sister, Angel, saw a photograph that had fallen out of it. The photograph was one of Luis I had forgotten about and she became very upset. My mother took me aside and explained what he had done to her and until that moment, I had no idea. I still did not understand what she meant, as the same thing had happened to me, and I did not ever know that it was wrong. You see, no one knew that Luis had done the same to me. But, I said nothing. I just agreed to throw the photograph away. I am confused a little on some of my memories. I still am to this day, really. My memory of most of it is gone and I try to remember, I do…but I don't think I really want to.

# MY NEXT STEP IN LIFE

August 14, 2014, my life took yet another turn. It is complicated. But, a special man came into my life. This man, who had been a close friend, asked my mother to join us for dinner at Chili's. He wanted to ask her permission to be my boyfriend. I was hesitant at first, because I had just gotten out of a relationship and I did not want people to think anything bad of me. I didn't care though, there was and has always been something special about Nate. So, I said yes. Things moved quickly, but he had told me he hadn't wanted anyone else to have the opportunity to catch me before he could. I hated sleeping by myself, so after a few months I asked him to stay with me for a little while. It was like a whirlwind romance falling for one another and being so close. Needless to say, he never left. Almost five years together this August and I couldn't be happier. Nate is my rock. He honestly is, and things could not be better with us.

But, now I want to share with you something beautiful, something rare, and something so pure yet, sad beyond anything one could ever imagine and you may say, how did you go on with life?

# MEET OUR DAUGHTER, MIA, TOO BEAUTIFUL FOR EARTH

It was February 22, 2017. My life was about to change, and I had no idea exactly how…but I had a feeling in my gut that something was wrong. I was a few weeks away from delivery. I had awakened, like every other day. But, this morning, something was not right, I could not feel Mia. She was quiet, not moving about as she usually had, happy for a new day.

I did not want to panic or freak everyone out, so, I called my nurse, and she calmly told me to go to the women's part of the hospital. I had a bad feeling, but I didn't want to alarm Nate or my mom. The medical team had been waiting for me when I arrived and they immediately began trying to find the fetal heartbeat. My nurse's face seemed reassuring at first, but then a couple of other nurses came in, followed by an ultrasound technician, who wouldn't look at me but my doctor finally arrived. Quietly he said he was sorry for our loss. A part of me wanted to yell out, Loss? Can't you do something…Anything?

The doctor said it was too late. My heart dropped into my stomach and Nate came to me. We were both broken, crying, and apologizing. I had never seen him so upset. I couldn't help to think it was my fault. What had I done wrong? What could I have done to change this? It seemed forever until they took me into the back room, though it was only a few minutes. That afternoon my doctor came in and gave me two options, I could give birth to Mia vaginally but, I'd have to get the epidural, and it would take about a day and a half to induce labor. My second option was to have a C-section. She explained to me all the risks, and told me the vaginal birth was the smarter choice of the two. I tried to explain that I couldn't go through the time and the trauma of giving birth to my daughter just to have nothing in return. I was scheduled that night for a C-section.

I hugged and cried with our family members on both my side and Nate's. It was time for my surgery.  I placed my hand on my stomach right before I went into the cold, white sterile surgical room, and I whispered I'm sorry, and that everything would be okay. I remember everything. I was awake and in total sorrow. I felt like I needed to see her, and at least touch her, to know that she was really there all that time I had carried her, spoken to her, and sang to her. I needed to see her. I silently prayed for the strength to get through this and to be strong for Nate and my mom.

A photographer came to take complimentary photographs of her time in the world. They brought Mia to me, in a little pink and purple crochet dress and beanie, wrapped in a blanket. She was perfect, with a head full of hair like mommy and daddy's…perfect lips and that stubborn nose I didn't like at first, but she was beautiful. Nate held her, while the photographer took the pictures. Mia looked like she was just sleeping. I prayed to God for her to just wake up. But nothing happened. They took her after a while. I wanted to remember her like I held her, peacefully sleeping, too beautiful for this world. I didn't want to see her cold or stiff. I couldn't. I stayed in the hospital for the following few days. The pain from the incision was unbearable. I couldn't walk or even cough. One night, Nate asked the nurse if he could see Mia one more time. He asked if I wanted to come, but I couldn't do it again. I tried to remember her as she was. Nate understood, and the nurse took Mia into a room where Nate could be alone with her. After about 30 minutes, Nate came back with tears in his eyes, hugged me, and we cried together.

We'll get through this, please don't leave me, I need you. He told me. Now more than ever. I couldn't imagine going anywhere. I couldn't imagine doing this without him, and I assured him of that. Time heals wounds, but it doesn't make you forget. Time doesn't take the pain away completely. I had to understand that things happen for a reason. It took me a long time because what kind of reason could there possibly be for my baby dying? I had to walk out of the hospital seeing all the new mommies with their babies. But, not me.

I see women abuse, or ignore, their children and I can't help but say something. They don't realize how lucky they are. They're blessed to have their children, and they're treating them like they don't matter. I would give anything to have Mia with me here today.

I must say I was extremely grateful for my best friend Samantha. She was there for me on one of the worst days of my life, and she was actually the one who helped my mom set up the go fund me for Mia's cremation. She's been by my side since the 7th grade as though we were of one heart and mind. I feel blessed to have her in my life.

*My name is Monica Montgomery. I was 21 years old as of December 20, 2015, when I first began to write my thoughts down, in an effort to share my story with you. If you are considering giving up on life because it's become a bit tough, don't even think it! Now, is the time to step up and fight back for the life you want and take control of it. You can turn it around. I ask you here and now to listen. Reach out to anyone who will listen, and more importantly, rely on your inner strength to be what you want in life. There is always a way to turn it around if You Never Give Up.*

*It's a Monday morning, (2015) and I'm sitting at a Starbucks at 5:00 am waiting to clock into work at 8:00 am. Why so early you say? My new car was totaled by some idiot texting and not paying attention. So here, I wait. Babe's dad drove us to work. You're probably thinking to yourself, babe? Work? I have not gone into too much detail regarding my life as a younger adult, have I? During this time in my life, I was rolling burritos at Chipotle. I have a brother and a sister, which you already know about. And babe? That's my Nate. He's amazing, he really is and he is my best friend being everything you could ask for and more. We had been through so much in the short four years that we had been together but now, Now, in our fifth year, we are still going strong.*

Lets talk about my mom, her name is also Mia. She was adopted when she was three years old by a large family and she loved her parents, though her mother was abusive and pretty much made her the housekeeper. Like the story of Cinderella, my mom was also terrified of her. She grew up with many brothers and sisters, so aside from the abuse, she had a pretty good childhood. In high school, mom had a short little afro and huge glasses. You know the kind. She was voted the most favorite person, most likely to succeed, and she was really into basketball and cheerleading. She was nonetheless, adorable in spite of being involved in so many physical activities.

*Mia, My Momma*

*She is my purpose and my why in life. She is my best friend and I will spend my life doing my absolute best to repay her for the horrific life she saved me from. My mom is the strongest person I know and she taught me my values. We've been through hell and back but she always reminds me that it'll be okay. God does not put us through anything we are incapable of handling.*

*Your Loving Daughter,*
*Monica*

Through everything we've been through, my mom is the strongest person I know. Her determination and love for us could save the world. When we endured the hard times, homeless, or living in battered women's shelters, my mom always told us that…Everything happens for a reason, and God has a plan for us. She made me the person I am today. She is my hero.

There have been several roadblocks and also many happy memories that I have shared along with you my journey in life. Most of my life has been a struggle. Some of those challenges would make the average person scream, toss their arms up, and crawl away in desperate attempts to quit. But, I have prevailed with holding on to the hope that my life had better roads ahead.

And it has. I soon began to realize that as human beings, we should not simply aspire to make a living, we should aspire to make a difference.

My life has now allowed me to become a mentor to others. Never did I imagine I would go from working at Chipotle to holding one of the highest levels of leadership with a company that I whole heartedly believe in. My job is to locate, train, develop leaders, and help them to achieve their full potential. I couldn't be more grateful for the opportunity. I have begun to think differently about my life, and you can do the same. But, you must remember to maintain a mindset that you will never ever quit. You must have a lust for life and believe it will be exactly as you want it to be.

The last thing I want to talk to you about is your WHY. Finding your reason why, your purpose is essential if you want to achieve higher levels of success. Your why must be greater than your excuses. If you do not have a strong enough reason behind your actions, your actions are less likely to create quality results. If your why is strong enough, you'll have all the fuel you need to drive you forward to your goals. So, what is your why? Make sure you know what it is. Set your goals in baby steps and set them further out each time you achieve the ones before. Push your comfort zone until you can't anymore…then push again! For me…my next step is to push forward to unveiling my lost, and painful past memories and publishing them in my up-coming book in 2020.

Always remember, it's not about where we come from, what matters is where we're going.

# For more information  please visit Monica's website at www.MonicaTheAuthor.com

# What Does Change Mean to You?

## Fundamental Elements for a Vibrant, Fulfilling Life

TONY DEBOGORSKI

How do you view change? For many individuals, change has become something to fear. It invokes feelings of anxiety and potential loss. There is often little focus on what we can gain from change. Instead, the negative feelings and thought patterns overwhelm us, which can make change more difficult to accept and benefit from.

Think of the flight or fight response. Change, if we don't manage it effectively, can trigger that response. It can make us respond as if our lives are being threatened, when it's more likely that we are simply being affected by changing circumstances. Some of these circumstances are in our control and others are out of our control. However, if we can alter our reaction to change, then we can reap some amazing benefits.

Yes, you can benefit from change. However, in order to do so you need to be willing to create a new mindset in regards to how you view change and how you choose to act. Without the right mindset, you might be missing out on a change that could give depth to your life and the lives of those around you.

Changes, both those that happen to us and the ones that we create ourselves, have the potential to create new opportunities and experiences we might otherwise miss. These can give us another perspective and enrich our lives. Change did just that for me as a young man.

I grew up in rural Canada, where hard work and sweat were the building blocks of your success. I learned to be a jack of all trades, because that was the way you got things done around a farm. When I left to attend university, the idea was that I would end up coming home, marrying my high school girlfriend, and raising my family in the farming community where I was raised.

This step towards a university education was already a big change, since only a few of my family members actually went on to get a university education. Working hard was our way of life, and it was hard physical work. I couldn't imagine any other way, but university gave me a new way to live and introduced me to the idea of working smarter, not harder.

My life was enriched by not only the classes I attended, but the people I met. I was exposed to those who hadn't lived their entire life on a farm.

I was exposed to different perspectives on how to tackle a variety of challenges. It altered my perception of the world, giving me a broader viewpoint. At the same time, I also deepened my appreciation of the values my parents instilled in me.

It was my first experience with change, but definitely not my last. I took the step to open my mind to change, which allowed me to get comfortable with the idea. During this time, I learned that it was okay to find assistance in accepting a change and acting on it without fear. The life I live today is defined by change. Now, instead of fear and anxiety, I welcome change for the blessings it may bring. How did I get to this point? It started with my willingness to learn and grew from there.

There is a process to change, but if we are not careful, we can actually prolong the process and make it more difficult. Let's walk through the reality of change. First, you have the old status quo. This is the reality of how things are right now. It could be a fairly peaceful way of life or you could find it difficult, but it is what you know.

Now a foreign element is introduced. It could be a new job or a move, for example. Most of the time, our first reaction is to resist, fearing the chaos that we are sure is to follow. After a point, we see the transforming idea of change and begin to integrate it into our lives. As time goes on, we then integrate the change into our lives and thus create a new status quo. Still, the impact of many aspects of this process can be lessened if we take a different point of view toward change.

Through mentors and my own experiences, I learned the key elements that can impact your ability to not only weather change, but thrive in the process. These five key elements are necessary to create the right mindset, one that embraces change, instead of being governed by a fear of change.

## KEY #1. SELF-BELIEF

The first key is your belief in yourself. This is the foundation of a vibrant and fulfilling life. Without confidence in your own ability to handle challenges, you will see change as a crisis, instead of a benefit or an opportunity to grow as an individual.

Throughout our lives, we are told how to act, dress, and even think. Our belief systems are influenced by this training. In addition, as we grow older and other influences come into play from the world around us. Just take a moment and think about all the people and ideas you encounter on a daily basis. These could be teachers, family members, workmates, television, the internet, etc. The list goes on and on.

All of these influences are not focused on teaching us to think for ourselves, but instead are focused on developing our thinking to fall in line with who they believe we should be. Call it the social conditioning of our world. There often isn't time to learn who we are, to spend time with ourselves, to think, imagine, and explore the world. Instead, if we don't buy out the time, we can find that we are dissatisfied with our lives and unable to determine why.

We often have our purpose in life defined for us by others. This can lead to a lack of fulfillment in our lives, especially if what we are supposed to be doesn't fit our true vision of who we are.

The key is to stop and examine your belief system. Focus on your values.

How many of them would you say you genuinely believe and how many have you taken on because of someone else in your life? It is amazing how many of our beliefs may no longer be serving us, but we are still using them to define ourselves and the world around us. Like the traditional fall and spring cleaning of our homes, we need to constantly be willing to clean the beliefs that no longer serve us or contribute to the growth and happiness of our lives from our consciousness.

Do you wake up in the morning satisfied with where you are in life? Can you look in the mirror and see a face excited to meet the day? Do you feel accountable for your life or does it feel as if your life is happening to you? How you see the world is based on your self-belief. What crafts your self-belief?

It hinges on your ability to see yourself master a skill and then be able to do it again and again successfully. Positive experiences help us grow our confidence in ourselves and define who we are. These moments often start in our early childhood, setting up a pattern throughout our lives.

My first memory of confidence building occurred when I was 11 years old. The regional elementary track and field meet was coming up. I wanted to win the top male athlete award. Although I had participated in the meet in the past, I hadn't won before. This time, I decided to do things differently. In preparation for the meet, I spent extra time training, including running after school. I was determined and my goal dominated my thoughts. It was a type of visualization, one that helped build my confidence going into the meet.

I had entered into five events and there were points for coming into first, second, and third place. On the day of the meet, it was sunny, the field and track were dry. Conditions were perfect for this outdoor event. My focus was on doing my best to earn the most points possible. At the end of the event, I had four first place ribbons and one for second place. I was presented with the trophy for top male athlete. That feeling of accomplishment boosted my sense of what I could do and built my self-belief.

What goals have you set that you were able to accomplish on your own? How did you feel after you achieved your goal? Setting and accomplishing goals is a great way to feel better about yourself. How does this translate into having a different mindset about change? When you feel confidence in your abilities, you will not find yourself fearing change and the challenges it can present.

However, in the midst of a major change, you might find yourself neglecting your needs. How often do we put ourselves last when others around us are in need of our time and attention? While we might think that it will last for only a short period of time, putting ourselves on the back burner can become a routine, one that has a negative impact on our lives.

This can leave you worn out mentally and put you into a negative frame of mind. I can point to research and personal experiences to give you examples of why a negative mindset can be the anti-change and can encourage you to avoid thinking about the potential benefits of change. Once you focus on caring for your needs, you are in a better position to weather change and give assistance to others. Once you find confidence and strength in yourself and your abilities, you will be able to master whatever change and challenges come your way.

One important point is that you might still be afraid, but don't let it paralyze you into not acting at all. Remember those moments of success and allow them to motivate you to keep going. The keys to being self-reliant are perseverance, dedication, and integrity. When you have them, you will be able to conquer just about anything.

# KEY #2. PURPOSE

Your life is a journey and you are the navigator. Some individuals choose to navigate based on their surroundings, essentially letting the waves aimlessly lead them along. In the end, that kind of life rarely leads to happiness with change or with yourself. You become a product of your circumstances, instead of defining yourself on your own terms.

What is purpose? According to the American Heritage Dictionary, it is "The object toward which one strives or for which something exists, an aim or a goal. The reason for which anything is done, created or exists, an aim or a goal."

When you examine your own life, are you excited about what you do? Could you define the purpose of your life? For some, their purpose becomes apparent when they are young. They find the passion that defines their lives and shapes their careers. Others never find that purpose, leaving them to struggle to find satisfaction with their lives.

If you haven't defined the purpose of your life, then it is time to think about what you enjoy. What sparks your passion? What gets you excited to get out of bed in the morning? Once you start to define your purpose, set your goals around what you enjoy. This can help you gain perspective on your purpose.

However, keep in mind that your purpose is not set in stone. It can change over time as you gain life experience and a better understanding of yourself. Taking action will help you be drawn to what you like. Try new things. Consider the spiritual influences in your life. To postulate is the act of creation. It can happen when you think, write, or speak something into being. Focus, because if you think it, then you can do it.

Change can be initiated by you. It doesn't have to be dominated by circumstances outside of your control. You can start by taking one action that will move you closer to a specific goal. That goal could be to simply change your way of thinking or to release a belief that is no longer serving you, but could be limiting you instead.

With your purpose defined, you could move forward to produce the life you want and mindset for change, which starts with how you take care of yourself.

## KEY #3. HEALTH

Fear and anxiety can have physical repercussions. They impact how our bodies feel, as well as our ability to fight off illnesses and deal with chronic conditions. Research has proven time and again that our minds can influence our physical well-being.

Are you poisoning your body through the negative thoughts you are dwelling on? To create the energy necessary for a vibrant fulfilling life you need to maximize your mental state, maintain your physical body, and nourish yourself properly. Keep your mind focused on what is possible, instead of focusing on what can't be done or any potentially negative consequences.

The combination of your mind and body is a synergistic relationship. It means you need to take care of both to achieve overall well-being. To start, let's focus on your physical body. Are you getting out on a regular basis to exercise and stretch your muscles? Do you raise your heart rate? One of the interesting side effects of physical activity is how it can impact our mood. When we are uplifted in mood, it translates into our thought processes. Regular physical exercise can contribute to greater overall positivity in our lives.

If you find it hard to get out on your own and get physically active, then consider finding a support group, a partner, or even a gym where you can be held accountable for showing up and putting in the effort. You will appreciate the results in terms of your health, making it worth the effort. Additionally, the physical benefits will allow you to grow in other areas of your life, thus making change more welcome, especially as your body grows stronger.

When it comes to your physical well-being, the reality is that you are what you put into your body. If you don't fuel your body for optimal performance, then it can't give you the very best physically. That can have a domino effect on how you operate mentally. When you are tired and not feeling your best, can you honestly say that you have made your best decisions? Or do you find yourself rethinking those choices at a later date?

There are five products, which I refer to as the five white poisons, that you need to be aware of. They can be found in a variety of foods throughout your local grocery store. So much of what we eat today has been processed extensively, removing the natural nutrients and fiber-rich parts. As a result, we are exposed to more of these five products than ever before. What are these five white poisons? Sugar, starch, flour, salt, and milk.

All of these are foods that need to be consumed in moderation. Recognize that they are often hidden ingredients within other foods. Therefore, it is wise to limit your intake wherever possible to make sure you aren't putting too much of these items into your body.

Part of your physical health is also caring for your brain. Think of it as a muscle. Like every muscle in your body, it is important to allow it to relax and get the necessary rest. This can be done through meditation or even finding some quiet time away from your family and friends to relax and think quietly without distraction. Doing so also allows you to reduce your stress level. Making sure your stress level comes down will positively impact your mental health as well.

Do you have a place that brings you peace? Having this place allows you to mentally unwind and just let go of your stress, even if it is just temporarily. Meditation is a method that you can use, even if all you can do is go to a quiet place in your home or office. There are a variety of meditation techniques available. Some individuals prefer a calming form of music to accompany their meditation, while others prefer to just enjoy the silence. Whatever you prefer, the point is to make your mental health a priority. If you do, it will be much easier to handle change and thrive.

Change can bring benefits and give us opportunities we might not otherwise have considered without the upheaval in our lives. But in order to benefit from change, we need to maintain our positivity, both physically and mentally. This can be hard to do when a change has a particularly emotional impact. Relying on family and friends for support is key to dealing with the more emotional aspects of any change in your life.

Throughout this discussion of your health, I haven't really touched on one area that impacts our well-being. That is our relationships. But how do they impact our lives and what do we need to remember about these relationships when it comes to change?

# KEY #4. RELATIONSHIPS

Did you know that you are shaped by the people you spend the most time with? Those individuals will influence your ideas, beliefs, and actions. This also extends to your attitude. If you are surrounded by positive thinkers, it is much easier to maintain a positive attitude. Think about the last time you were surrounded by negative individuals. After a while, did it seem as if that negative and critical spirit rubbed off on you?

Here are some questions to ask yourself about the people you spend time with. Are they primarily positive or negative? Do you find yourself having spirited conversations with plenty of give and take, or do you find that you are just a dumping ground for all their complaints about life?

If you want to create change in your life or be more accepting of the changes in your life, then you may need to assess who you spend most of your time with. Creating a new attitude or shifting your thought process means assessing who is influencing them both and whether that influence is helping or hurting.

When I was finishing my university education, I was associating with a group of friends who were eager to join the corporate world. I had worked in the corporate world during my summer breaks, but I had also started a business installing sprinkler systems in areas where there was new home construction. I did this after hours and on weekends. Although I was working a lot, I was also figuring out that I didn't have to go the corporate route to be successful. My small part-time business had made me more money than my daily corporate job.

Our final year of school came and, of course, my friends and I discussed what our next steps were as we started life after university. Some had mixed feelings about what direction to take after graduating. The options included attempting to open a business in the role of entrepreneur or applying to one of the many companies out there for a traditional corporate role.

Since most of my friends decided to go the corporate route, I did too, even though my experience indicated that I could be equally, if not more, successful in the role of entrepreneur. The individuals I associated with provided acknowledgement and support during that decision-making period of my life.

Are there some decisions where you can see the influence of your associates? Can you look back now and see that perhaps a different decision would have been more appropriate for the path you ultimately wanted to pursue?

While we all want to think that we are independent thinkers, sudden influences from our associates can impact what we choose to do and how we think and act. Yet, with a greater understanding of who you are as a person (your goals and your passions), you will find that you can truly be an independent thinker and identify the effect of those influences around you.

Self-knowledge takes time, but the reward is a better way to embrace life and the change around us, both personally and professionally. If you want to move down a specific path toward your goal, you need to make sure to associate with like-minded individuals. They can encourage and support you as you work to achieve those specific milestones.

As you discover what you are passionate about, you will be able to find like-minded friends and associates who are focused on that particular activity or pursuit. For instance, you may be passionate about helping young people. There may be local groups geared toward providing activities and mentorship to teenagers within your community. Getting involved in those groups will put you around others who share your passion, which can help motivate you even further.

Take the time to examine your beliefs and determine if the friends you are associating with are the right people to support you in the next stage or season of your life. Not everyone you spend time with will be an active part of helping you achieve your goals. However, they can be the individuals who make you laugh, as well as help you see the positive when situations or circumstances seem overwhelming.

The point is to be around people who embrace change and can help you to do the same. When it comes to your mindset, negative association will eventually bring even the most positive mindset down. Have you ever tried to accomplish something that you had already decided was impossible? It becomes an uphill battle, and you likely didn't succeed.

A positive attitude, on the other hand, makes it possible for you to achieve even more than you thought was possible. In addition, your positive mindset could have an influence on those around you. Imagine being a positive influence to those who are important to you. The best relationships are the ones where you both are actively working to support and encourage each other in pursuit of your passions, while being there for each other during times of major change or upheaval that life seems to throw at us all.

If you are looking to make adjustments to your circle of friends and associates, consider looking into your community for opportunities to meet new people. Some ideas include joining a club or charity organization. If there is an activity that you have been interested in trying, why not sign up for lessons? What things have you been afraid to try for one reason or another? Why not give one of those things a try? If your fear is that you won't do well, make peace with that and do it anyway. You might find that as you conquer your fear, you make new friends that will enrich your life.

I want to point out here that the idea is to make you better able to adapt to change and train yourself to see the benefit of change versus focusing on the fear and anxiety. Each of these new experiences is putting you in charge of creating change in your life on a smaller scale, which will make it easier for you to handle change on a larger scale.

The most rewarding sport even for me was signing up and participating in triathlons. I was a prairie boy who didn't grow up around water. Signing up for a triathlon forced me to learn how to swim. I could have let fear of the unknown stop me, but instead I broadened my horizons.

Additionally, I signed up with a friend. We challenged each other and held each other accountable for attaining our goals. It was not an easy journey, but I found new strength as I pushed myself and supported my friend.

The 10-month journey before my first triathlon was grueling at times. It included swim lessons, getting the proper equipment, the proper bike, the right shoes, and more. After those 10 months of training, lessons, and standing up to my own fears, the day of the race finally came.

The first leg of the triathlon was swimming, which I can definitely say was not my strength. In fact, when I ran into the water, I was with a pack of men, but after a few minutes of kicking and banging around, I was alone and about ready to give up. Instead of doing that, I pulled back for a moment, composed myself, and then started to swim, concentrating on one stroke at a time.

I finished dead last in the swim, but at least I finished. I continued with ease to do the bike and run, completing those two legs in top times. I was dead last overall, because of my slow swim, but I still felt a great sense of accomplishment because I had completed my goal. In the process, I had met many new people who shared an interest in triathlons. I also got closer to my friend Nick, who trained with me and completed the same triathlon.

It was a rewarding event for me, not only because I actually finished what I set out to do, but because when I went out to celebrate that night, I met my future wife. Our relationship has been full of change and challenges, but none of the joys would have been possible if I hadn't stepped outside of my comfort zone to try something new and conquered a fear at the same time.

Think about the various relationships in your life. Could there be someone who is already in your life who would be supportive as you step outside your comfort zone? Those individuals are the ones who will support you through change. They are key relationships to nurture. Still, those relationships will not be able to support you if you are not able to communicate your needs to those critical people in your life. As a result, my fifth key is also the most critical: communication.

# KEY #5. COMMUNICATION

No matter who we are and what we do throughout the day, we are constantly communicating. We use our faces, our hands, and, of course, our speech to communicate what we are thinking and feeling on a daily basis.

Yet within the realm of communication, the opportunities for misunderstandings abound. There are literally hundreds of thousands of examples throughout history demonstrating how misunderstandings can grow into much larger breakdowns of relationships between individuals, groups, and even countries.

Communication is truly an incredible concept. Great communicators can wow us and bring difficult concepts or ideas into focus. Have you ever heard the speeches of Martin Luther King Jr.? Decades after his passing, his words continue to move people. Then there are more current examples, such as Tony Robbins, Bob Proctor, or Brian Tracy. All of these individuals are amazing in their delivery of self-help information. Listen to their presentations and you can see how they really connect with their audiences.

Change requires communication, but change doesn't go over well if it is not communicated well. Every parent who communicates with a teenager can appreciate this point. Their child may not be able to articulate their frustration or the reasons behind it. An argument often becomes par for the course, leaving everyone frustrated and out of sorts. Misunderstandings can make change difficult to handle, because you may not understand why the change is occurring.

Companies often make this mistake as well. They may not clearly communicate their vision, so when they make changes, their employees are often left feeling frustrated and out of the loop. It can also make them feel uncertain about their job security, which can negatively impact their productivity. The reality is that miscommunication can have a large impact on whether change is welcomed or feared.

Communication is more than just speaking clearly. It is listening to and understanding the concerns of the other person and doing your best to address those concerns. When it comes to creating change in your life, you may find that you need to explain to your family why you are making that change. How do you communicate your choice? Often, how well it is communicated is reflected in the level of support you receive and if the change is embraced or not.

Have you been part of a change where the communication was less than you expected? How did that impact your ability to accept the change and create something incredible from that opportunity? For many of us, the answer is that the change was more difficult and we likely didn't support it wholeheartedly.

Again, the point is that communication can make a change easier to accept or a lack of it can make the implementation of a change more difficult. If you are initiating change in your own life, be sure that you are clearly communicating your needs to those around you. While they may not always agree with your decisions, they are much more likely to support them and the changes you want to make if you can clearly communicate the change and its impact.

Along with good communication, you need to be a good listener. Often misunderstandings occur because one individual is not really listening to the other. They may miss key instructions or details that could make the situation clearer. As a result, it can be easy to act without truly knowing all the necessary facts and circumstances. Can you see how not listening well could impact how you feel about a change in your life? It is also easy to see how others might be less supportive of change you initiate if they weren't listening.

How can you tell if someone is truly hearing you? Ask them questions and then clarify when it appears that they may not have gotten an accurate picture of what is about to occur. Some individuals may want to willfully misunderstand, and you want to do everything in your power to avoid that. At the same time, be a good listener. Don't listen to respond, but listen to understand their concerns, worries, and potential fears. Make adjustments to address their concerns where possible, but be as reassuring as you can when those adjustments might not be possible.

When you don't listen, you run the risk of missing key instructions or information that could directly impact your life or the change you are about to make.

I was always working, even from a young age. For a period of time, I worked on a gravel crusher as a ground person. My job was to go around and check for broken wheels, conveyors, and signs of wear and tear on other components. If something was wrong, I was to report it immediately to the tower person overseeing the operation. His job was to shut down the entire mechanical operation so the problem could be addressed. If he didn't, a major failure could occur, which could end up costing thousands of dollars of damage.

One morning, I was tired and didn't pay attention when I was relieving the previous shift. I had missed that a flashing was tearing and did not report it. An hour later, that flashing tore through. My boss saw it first. Gravel was everywhere. He had the operation stopped, then came over to the tool shack to fire me for not properly checking the system. That miscommunication cost the company time and money, plus I lost my job. The lesson? Communication and paying attention to the details is key to success in any area of your life, but especially when you are initiating major change.

Now let's talk about how a lack of communication can contribute to conflict. Our ability to connect with others can be hampered if we don't communicate well or if we are not sensitive to their needs and hot spots. Our personal and professional lives can be impacted by poor communication.

If you are considering acting to make changes in your life, start with how you communicate with others. We can all find areas to improve and make our connections with others deeper and more meaningful. The art of language is not easy. From birth, we are trained to communicate, but it doesn't come easily to all of us. Some become better than others at expressing themselves. The art of communication can be terrifying and amazing at the same time. You may also find it difficult to express yourself, especially when dealing with loved ones. How can you communicate more effectively with the individuals in your life?

Start by asking questions. This helps you gather information. Repeat back to the speaker your understanding of what they just said in response to your question. If they don't agree with your interpretation, keep asking for clarification until you get it. Be sure that you genuinely listen to the response before you start making assumptions. Try and imagine the situation from the other person's point of view. Be patient, because the best communication takes time.

There are also classes on public speaking and the art of communication. If you find yourself struggling consistently in this area, consider taking a course. The principles and real-world practice can help you improve your general communication skills. If you find yourself losing your train of thought, then consider writing down what you want to say. Be clear and concise where possible. Then use your written thoughts as a platform to bring up various points when appropriate within the context of the conversation.

Don't underestimate the power of practicing your communication skills in front of a mirror. This is where you can work on eye contact, exploring your various facial expressions, and also how to speak clearly. If you can talk to yourself, then it will get easier to talk to others. Make an effort to come out of your comfort zone, especially if you are not a good communicator. Consider it a change for the better.

Recognize that by improving your communication skills you can improve the quality of your life, as well as weather changing circumstances more effectively.

## MOVE FORWARD WITH ME

Throughout this chapter, I have focused on some key areas that can make change more palatable, and reduce the fear and anxiety that commonly occurs. Still, the reality is that change, especially change we didn't initiate, can be overwhelming. Over the course of my lifetime, I have dealt with a variety of changes and I can say that not every experience was pleasant. But they all taught me valuable lessons.

I also want to remind you that change doesn't need to be something that occurs to you, but can be something you initiate. Consider areas of your life that are not as satisfying as you would like them to be. For example, are you struggling financially, but find yourself reluctant to make changes or take the risks necessary to turn your financial life around? Here is an area where making a change happen can have a significant impact.

However, don't limit yourself merely to material affluence. There are literally dozens of areas where you could find yourself hesitating to make changes. No matter what change you want to make, the mindset you choose will determine whether the change is successful or a struggle.

Throughout my work with individuals on changes in their lives, one thing has become clear; your mindset is key to making change work for you and allowing yourself to embrace change effectively.

I'm willing to work with you to help create the change that you want to see in your life. Let's face it, changes to our self-belief can lead to even more significant changes in other areas of our lives. With an improvement to your self-belief, there is no telling what you can accomplish. The changes to your point of view about yourself and what you can accomplish will help you make different choices about how you choose to live and work.

I believe that coaching is key to creating the right mindset to initiate and absorb changes in your life. A positive mindset allows you to see change in terms of what is possible, instead of focusing on the potential losses. Until you take the leap, you will never know exactly what is possible. But it can be hard to take those first steps to overhauling your thought process on your own.

I believe strongly in coaching and mentorship. It is a way to pass on the wisdom you have learned and the key strategies you may have discovered for addressing and initiating change. As part of my efforts to help others embrace change, my coaching and mentorship is available to you.

In my book, The Book of Change, I tackle a variety of topics and areas where you can start making small changes to build up to bigger ones. I also discuss how you can take dramatic and difficult circumstances and use them to learn and grow.

Using these tools, you can make a difference in your own life and in the lives of others. You can go from being fearful of change to being an example of embracing change for those in your family, your social circle, and your community. However, coaching isn't the only way to work on your skills to create and embrace change.

You can become a change advocate. That means allowing your positive mindset regarding change to influence others and impact their attitudes toward possible changes in their own lives. Your own example of dealing with change can serve as inspiration for others, which can then allow them to turn themselves into change advocates. It is a never ending cycle, which can give you peace of mind, even when faced with the toughest of challenges.

Additionally, there are other key takeaways for you to keep in mind as you start the journey to create change in your life. One way to embrace it is to understand what is happening and even to learn why.

Continuing education allows you to take the fear out of any change. After all, most of the fear of change stems from a lack of knowledge about what the change will mean for you, your family, and your community. When we are informed, change can be less intimidating, which can make us less fearful and more willing to take risks. Change is a part of taking risks to grow and explore our passions, achieve our goals, and fulfill our dreams. Without the right information and mindset, we will be unwilling to take the risks needed to achieve everything we imagine possible.

Clearly, you need to remember that change is a constant in your life. No one can escape it, no matter how risk adverse they may be. You need to embrace change for the benefits it can provide by creating a different mindset, gaining new skills, or even just acknowledging the personal growth that has resulted.

The change you see in your lifetime can and likely will have a profound impact on the lives of others, both now and in the future. Respect the people around you and demonstrate love and support when they are faced with changes, both large and small.

Contact me at **tony@tonydebogorski.com**. I would love to explore the ways that I can help you create real change in your life through adjustments to your mindset and increasing your willingness to learn and explore. Be inspired to create the meaningful life that you have always wanted and step away from living in fear of the unknown.

Amazing things are waiting for you! It is time for you to take the first step towards being a change agent in your own life.

# Perspective Thinking

ANDREA NGUI

Our experiences shape our perspectives. Yet, our perspectives also shape our experiences. It is a continual circle. Throughout my journey, I learned how shifting my perspective altered my experiences and opened the door to some amazing opportunities. Let me share my journey with you, as well as how shifting your perspective can help you change your life.

Often, the choices you make come down to your perspective and how it impacts your thinking. As an entrepreneur, I love the idea of breaking out of the status quo to create an amazing life. Taking that step to break my own status quo set me up to experience things and places I hadn't thought possible.

To me, the status quo is defined as settling for a corporate job, one where you spend your time making money for someone else. I have always wanted to be my own boss, but that dream had to be put on hold as I started working and gaining experience in various roles, including retail, restaurants, geographic information systems, and sales. I hopped jobs based on the money, but more importantly, I gained a lot of experience in many roles and won several awards. I focused on the material benefits, even though I wasn't focused on what type of career spoke to me.

Eventually, I realized there was more to my career than just making money. So, I asked myself what I wanted to do with the rest of my professional life.

Perhaps you have faced this situation in your own life. You know what you don't want to be doing with your career, but you haven't zeroed in on what you do want. Part of my early journey to break the status quo was understanding how my perspective influenced my thinking and my choices. I wasn't listening to my gut feelings or following my intuition. The result was that I allowed my thinking to be dominated by fears or the almighty dollar, instead of chasing my dreams. My perspective had been narrowed by the status quo that I was mindlessly following.

Things had to change as I faced some life-threatening challenges. To create the drastic change in my lifestyle, I had to start taking my health and happiness more seriously than I ever had before. One of the major challenges I live with is being seriously allergic to certain foods. I have dealt with multiple anaphylactic episodes, which meant that various jobs could expose me to life-threatening situations in a matter of moments. I needed to create a safer external environment to live in. Coping with my allergies to food isn't easy. I might as well live in bubble wrap. I could live in fear and keep myself from exploring new places and new experiences in an attempt to protect myself from everything that can harm me. It also made me realize that life can be over faster than expected. I decided to shift gears in figuring out how to start living my dream lifestyle, i.e. what makes me happy and healthy. This meant I had to gain clarity in my professional life.

Another major factor that I had to confront was chronic pain. I simply pushed myself more every day with what had to be done. I pushed my tolerance limits to the max, which meant I jeopardized my health and wellbeing. Shifting my perspective meant changing my approach. I had to figure out how to stop being overly focused on the future and, rather, focused on enjoying the present. Instead of pushing at full speed physically, I took time to relax by watching movies and listening to music. A benefit of taking this time for myself was that it also inspired my creativity.

Since so much of what I wanted was wrapped up in my health, I concentrated on that first and foremost. I visited many health practitioners, doctors, neurological clinic, conducted a CAT scan and MRI. All my results concluded my nervous system is functioning perfectly healthy. Nothing made sense. My body was constantly in pain. It was painful resting, walking, putting clothes on hangers, to swimming in the water. I found a network spinal analysis (NSA) chiropractor and increasing my physical fitness made the chronic pain permanently disappear. My chronic pain stemmed from life stressors.

I also started exercising to improve my physical endurance. Soon, I signed myself up for my first 5k and 10k road races. The benefits were not limited to physical ones. Those endorphins and the sense of accomplishment after each race spurred me to keep up my efforts.

I have also found that slowing down to take more time for self-care allows me to think with clarity. With a humbler and steadier attitude, I am no longer watching life bypass me, but instead I am enjoying life to the fullest. I am living my best lifestyle today, not later, because later may never come.

# SETTING GOALS AS PART OF THE SHIFT

One of the benefits of opening my mind and heart to perspective thinking is that I listen more spiritually to the universe, using its guidance to unfold my life.

Your perspective can make you feel as if you do not have control over what is happening in your life. Professionally, you can feel as if you are a hamster on a wheel, trapped in your personal status quo. Shifting your perspective can be challenging if you are not sure what direction you truly want to go. I was so busy chasing money that I wasn't focused on achieving the right career for myself. Once I stopped dreaming and started to take action in defining my life goals and the lifestyle I wanted to live, I came to the realization of what my life profession would become.

If you meet people who have achieved their life goals and created their ideal life, they all talk about the fact that they took action. They moved! Life goals are going to set the framework for your actions and choices. Recognize that your perspective throughout life is key to staying on track to achieve what you truly desire in life.

Life is going to throw curve balls and readjusting is a necessary part of reaching your life goals. Taking the time to move at a slower pace by allocating time and space to learn from and reflect on what you have already accomplished will help you continue setting milestones that get you closer to your goals.

Identifying your life goals means that you can start laying out a timeline with milestones to help you reach your goals. Take notice of the fact that you can plan milestones forever, but if you don't start moving and take that first step, then it will just remain a to-do list with nothing crossed off and accomplished.

Start with a smaller goal, just to get moving. After all, once you achieve that first small goal, it can be all the motivation you need to tackle the next one and build resilience and consistency as you encounter setbacks. The beauty of these small steps is that even with setbacks, what you already accomplished can give you the strength, inspiration, and courage to keep moving forward. Now let's talk about some of those setbacks or obstacles, especially those that you create within yourself.

# IDENTIFYING OBSTACLES TO SHIFT YOUR PERSPECTIVE

It is so easy to point the finger at your circumstances and the individuals around you as the reasons why you cannot move forward. You create reasons why you can't do something or why it is impossible. You may even blame others for your inability to accomplish your goals. The point is that those excuses and the blaming of others allows you to stay still and feel comfortable with not creating permanent change in your life. We've all heard the saying "Try, try, try again, and never give up." Perhaps giving up on your current direction by turning around into a new direction may just give you that zest feeling you long for in life. Moving forward isn't a straight line. In sports, players keep moving forward, but not always in a straight line, to get another touchdown, a basket, or a homerun.

Ask yourself, is it circumstances or an excuse that I am telling myself? Too often, our excuses block us from seeing the solutions that could be right in front of us. You need to get out of your own way. When you make excuses, you are creating barriers to dictate which way you should live.

Let's face it, self-inflicted fearmongering can be a big form of self-sabotage.

You can build up the fears in your mind to the point that you choose inaction instead of moving forward with courage.

Negative thinking can be encouraged or discouraged, depending on the thoughts you allow to be planted in your mind. You might feel like you are getting ahead, but the truth is that you are not really getting anywhere. Instead, you are simply stuck doing what you did yesterday, and if anyone points out to you that fact, then you have excuses for why you aren't progressing. You treat challenges as obstacles that cannot be overcome.

For instance, if you're dealing with a chronic health condition, you may have a tougher battle against negative thinking. After all, you are likely dealing with a variety of challenges, such as pain or limited range of motion. The physical limitations can be even harder to deal with if it impacts your independence. You can become exhausted, mentally and physically. Building a strong, healthier mindset will help you cope and potentially overcome your chronic health issue.

On the flip side, you can be the source of negative thinking for others and end up causing toxicity in someone else's thoughts. If you find yourself surrounded by those who talk negatively, stop for a moment and analyze how you are speaking. Are you drawing negativity to yourself? Shifting your perspective means being honest with yourself about the thoughts and words you allow yourself to use to describe yourself and others.

Part of changing or shifting your perspective involves power shifting your thoughts to lessen the impact of negative thinking. Once you start shifting your thinking, you will notice a breakthrough in defeating excuses and self-sabotage.

Another way to stop your negative thinking is to look at what you are feeding your brain in terms of social media. After all, there are arguments and differences of opinion that play out over the internet. You might have been in a good mood, but then you read something online and became instantly angry, even though nothing happened to you personally.

Have you ever been in a performance sports car? As the driver pushes on the gas pedal, the car can accelerate over 60 miles per hour in less than two seconds. Visualize your life performing like a sports car. If you don't push the gas pedal and tap into your power, then it is not going to perform like you anticipated. Constantly shifting your perspective as quickly as the speed of a performance sports car is key to learning what it takes to live a successful life.

Here is the important thing to remember before you can make any changes in your life. When changing your mindset, start with the invisible internal dialogue. This needs to occur before the visible external changes can properly manifest. The results of your thinking will be shown through your actions and decisions.

Your inner voice can often be one of the greatest challenges that you need to overcome to create change in your life. If you focus on thoughts based on fear, then you are going to end up becoming your own blockade. Your fear will constantly dictate what you do, trapping you in a place where you feel that everything around you is a huge risk. You could be living a fun and enjoyable life. All you need to do is conquer your fears. Always move forward with courage, even if you still feel the fear within you.

For instance, you might not like the life you are living, but it is the only one that you know. Fear might make you resist change, simply because you fear that you have so much to lose if you change. So why should you bother to make the effort? Essentially, you are self-defeating, even before you have tried or given change a chance.

Here is the reality that we all have to face. Change is coming regardless of whether we want it or not. While change can equate with loss or challenges, there is also much that can be gained.

Take a minute and look at a situation where you are fearful of change and losing what you have. Now, instead of focusing on what you might lose, let's shift to thinking about all that you might gain.

Instead of waiting for the world to bring joy and happiness into your world, start thinking about how you can create it on your own. This may include changing your routine or making a giant leap of change in your job or living situation. There are so many stories out there of individuals deciding to take a giant leap. Their experiences show how changing your thinking can allow you to make some amazing leaps in life. Your thinking can inspire you to act and make choices that align with the life you desire to live.

You need to figure out what type of life you want to live. Start focusing on what brings you joy. Often, it can be hard to separate the life that you want from the life that you are expected to live by society and your family. If you shape your life around the expectations of others, even your loved ones, then you are essentially disowning your true self for an imitation. Now, the process of letting go of those expectations and claiming the life you want to live does take effort.

How many times have you been in the position where you tried to do something and then tanked, such as a road race? Instead of crossing the finish line victoriously, you fell and twisted an ankle just a few feet past the starting line. Your perception of that experience can go one of two ways.

The first way is that you can look at that race and decide you will never run again. The second way is to look at that race and make a decision that you are going to learn from that experience. Perhaps you need different shoes, or another training regimen.

Notice that the second perspective was about finding the ways that you can learn from the experience, improve, and have a successful outcome the next time. That is a perspective that embraces learning, change, and growth. Training and practice are part of the journey.

To get to where you want to be, you need to have a clear vision of what type of life you want. Once you know where you want to be at a certain point, then you need to create an action plan around getting from point A to point B. When you create your action plan, it has to be wrapped around your perspective that it is possible to achieve.

Here is a quick exercise. Ask yourself what you tolerate from yourself that you might not tolerate in others and write it down. Remember, when you make an excuse, you are not holding yourself accountable in being true to yourself. How would you feel if you discarded things you tolerated? How would your life change?

You have to listen to your gut feelings. When you smother intuition, inertia kicks in and you get stuck with your decision making. Spend time to gain clarity with your mind to let yourself properly receive the message from your intuition.

When I was stuck in my status quo, doing the job and exhausting myself in the process, I realized that no one was going to be as concerned about my pursuit of happiness in living out my dream lifestyle than me.

No one is truly stopping you or standing in your way. The only person doing that is you! Recognize that other people will never truly understand what you need to do until you take action and they start to see the results.

Then they will understand more in-depth what you need to do and why you need to do it. Who knows? You might end up inspiring them to shift their own perspective and start creating something amazing in their own lives.

It is about designing the life you want to live. Acknowledge you deserve to live an amazing life. Become the leader of your own life destiny. Be your own hero and a role model to others.

Once I focused on creating that lifestyle which I had designed for myself, then I started to live the best years of my life. The radiant self-fulfilling lifestyle journey that I began creating for myself has been the most wonderful and marvelous experience, and I get to experience it every single day. The amount of peace and harmony that I know is so abundant. It motivates me to continue to achieve and focus on living this lifestyle that I desire and deserve to live. What you prioritize is what your life will reflect, so make sure you are prioritizing the things that bring you joy and happiness.

Everything that I have achieved started with changing my perspective and focusing on what was possible instead of labeling it as impossible. Now let's focus on how shifting your perspective can help improve your relationships with others.

# CREATING AMAZING RELATIONSHIPS IN YOUR LIFE

Relationships with individuals throughout your life are going to be complicated. You may find that someone challenges you, while another person provides unconditional support. As you are making amazing changes and shifts in your life, you need to shape your personal inner circle to find those who will challenge you and support you, even as you do the same for them.

Think about the people who surround you now. Do they support you on your journey of growth? Do they hold you accountable when you start to slip back into the status quo or that old way of thinking and behaving? If you want to create a major shift in your life, then you need those individuals to hold you accountable and to be honest with you.

Staying true to ourselves morally and ethically is not always easy when we surround ourselves with those who do not subscribe to our morals and ethics. Those within your inner circle are going to have the most profound impact on your thinking and actions.

As part of your journey to building your inner circle, it is important to clarify what you want to achieve in your life. Remember to focus on yourself. The best relationship, the best friendship you have, is the relationship you have with yourself. Self-mastery is key in figuring out how to live a purposeful life.

I embraced my dreams by initially writing them down. For example, I purchased my first home on my own, took a trip to Machu Picchu and the Galapagos Islands, and revolved my schedule around volunteering at events I always wanted to partake in. I achieved these dreams, but the timeframe was a lot longer than predicted.

Where do you want to go? What do you want to see and experience? The world is large and there are plenty of places to see, cultures to explore and experience, and food to try. Another benefit of traveling is that you build confidence in your abilities, be it to navigate travelling in a foreign country or conquering a mountain. Start crossing things off your bucket list or else you'll find yourself with a long list that was never accomplished.

Be open to new experiences and allow yourself to enjoy a variety of what life has to offer. It's the best way to truly discover yourself. It's time to stop existing and start living a fun and enjoyable life. When you purposefully plan the type of life you want and share with the world how you want to be treated, then people will respond.

Take a piece of paper and spend a few minutes thinking about everything that you want to accomplish in your life. Don't put timeframes on it. Goals and milestones move you forward in your life and can help you achieve what is necessary to transition through different life stages. A bucket list is based around experiences and moments that you want to have as part of your life's journey.

# CREATE FINANCIAL INDEPENDENCE

Another part of perspective thinking is homeownership. Some individuals have different ideas regarding owning property, but the truth is that homeownership is key to building your net worth.

Financially, I had to be frugal to accomplish my goals of becoming an entrepreneur and homeowner. When you have a greater purpose, a greater "why" for your shift in perspective, and a greater reason why you are doing what you are doing, then everything else becomes irrelevant.

Being worried about money and driven to make more can lead to an obsession at the level that you will ignore your loved ones, your health, and your well-being. I did exactly that, constantly burnt out to prove that I could make it in the corporate world. Keeping up an image that I didn't want to be known for.

You can move yourself forward financially if you take responsibility for your choices and take control of how you are using your assets. If it seems as if you are sabotaging yourself financially, then you might want to stop and explore your attitude regarding money. Often, your struggles to stay on budget, control your spending, or save to invest can be wrapped up in beliefs about money that have burrowed into your subconscious and become part of the spending choices you make on a daily basis.

The way money and financial matters were presented when you were younger impacts your financial perspective today. The last financial recession had a major impact on many families and their finances. For the people this affected, their goal now may be to take fewer financial risks to avoid having that experience happen to them again.

If you look back to those who grew up during the Great Depression, they often struggled to spend money on anything, even when they clearly needed it. These individuals had lived through traumatic financial experiences, so their future choices of not wanting to put money in banks or to live very frugally were understandable. If your grandparents were raised in that era, they may have passed some of those beliefs or fears onto you.

What are your beliefs about money? How you view money and the beliefs behind those views will help you to appreciate why you make certain financial decisions. If you don't figure out the underlying cause, you will be unable to fix it. Instead, you will simply manage the symptoms, which is not the best long-term solution.

## THE POWER IN WRITING

Throughout this chapter, you have learned the value in shifting your perspective. There are many fantastic opportunities in life if you explore with curiosity.

It is possible to heal from the past and move confidently into your future. Find ways to move, act, and create motion within your life. Working with a life coach can support you in your self-discovery journey. I help both men and women who are fitness enthusiasts and business owners to achieve their goals by focusing on successful habits, mindsets, wellbeing, nutrition, fitness, and relationships. I want to tell you that it is possible to heal from the past and live a better life starting today. You deserve to live your dream lifestyle now. Contact Andrea Ngui at www.herovi.coach.

Start by creating steppingstones to put yourself in a position to leap into the life you always wanted to live. Intention and deliberate actions are key to shifting your perspective.

Let's put perspective thinking into perspective. For example, whether it's a testimonial on LinkedIn, feedback on a report, a critique of a movie, a biography for a speaking engagement, or an opinion of a product on Amazon, they usually all have a more thoroughly written response than a verbal response. You know what I am saying?

Articulating your message by writing it down, or typing it out, has a profound effect on your level of perspective thinking. It helps heighten your level of awareness, level of learning, level of maturity, and level of wisdom. So, will you be writing things down on paper or on an electronic device?

Social media platforms are great tools in training your brain to ensure you are as articulate as possible with your message. Your message should be clear and concise with the knowledge you want others to read. You want to minimize the range of misinterpretation.

When it comes to complex things in life, how can you figure things out if you can't even articulate yourself proficiently by initially writing them down?

Don't get hung up on the agonizingly annoying feeling that the process will take too long. The length of time is irrelevant. Doing a half fast job leaves you stuck in a repetitive loophole with the illusion of the falsehood that you solved the issue. Writing it down and writing it out allows you to organize your thoughts. How can you expect to communicate clearly if you don't truly and entirely know what you want to say?

Expressing yourself by articulating your feelings with better words will help you get from where you are now to where you want to be. Eventually, it will help you create what you desire to achieve in life.

Creativity can be taught through perspective thinking. The television show Stranger Things has an upside-down world, which is another dimension of the universe. Songs, movies, quotes, clichés, and poetry all tend to have a deeper meaning than what the eye beholds on the surface. Has it ever happened to you when, over time, hearing the same clichés makes a new insight pop into your head? You start to wonder, "How did I miss that this entire time? I didn't know. I had no idea. Why didn't you tell me before?" Seeing things from another angle, from the inside out, and elevating your level of thinking helps you improve in becoming a problem solver within your own life.

Preparation is key in achieving the result of success. As Eric Thomas, aka ET, says, "Fall in love with the process, and the results will come." Practice makes perfect. Do the training, drills, exercises, practices, and show up where you really need to grind it out.

Is this why athletes practice so much? To fine tune their athleticism? Could this be a success method in how people accomplish so much in a day? A successful habit to develop is to intentionally think about embracing a continuous higher level of awareness with everything. It all starts with your level of perspective thinking. Life will start to unfold with what you deserve, and you will reap what you sow. Let this glimpse into how I shifted my perspective inspire you to do the same.

Contact Andrea Ngui at **www.herovi.coach** to learn how you can work together as you shift your perspective thinking and grow your business and personal lifestyle.